BASEBALL:

The Sports Playbook

Gil McDougald and Fred McMane

BASEBALL:
The Sports Playbook

Illustrations by Tony Pannoni
Special Photography by Dwight Johnson

Doubleday & Company, Inc.
Garden City, New York

PHOTO CREDITS:
Spectra Action, pages 11, 12, 13, 34, 54, 61, 64, 65, 66, 74, 82, 83, 84, 90, 98
Malcolm W. Emmons, pages 18, 27, 28, 46
Wide World Photos, 41

ISBN: 0-385-05913-2
Library of Congress Catalog Card Number 76–42346
Copyright © 1977 by Doubleday & Company, Inc.
Printed in the United States of America
All Rights Reserved
9 8 7 6 5 4 3 2

CONTENTS

INTRODUCTION

Though very much a team game, baseball is probably the most individually rewarding sport played in America. In many ways, any athletic activity compensates those who participate in it, particularly through the sense of exhilaration that comes from accomplishing a difficult feat at a crucial time in the contest. Run for the winning touchdown as the game-ending gun goes off, score the tie-breaking basket at the buzzer, put in the winning goal in sudden-death overtime—these are the Meriwellian acts that come to mind when one thinks of the sense of elation and achievement available to sports participants. Baseball offers these—and more.

Baseball offers a sense of accomplishment to the player who *thinks,* the player who *anticipates,* the player who thoroughly *understands the game.* Of course, you must be able to throw a baseball and catch it, know how to swing a bat and run bases, but these skills are basic. Armed with them, it still takes a great deal of know-how to play the game well—and that is precisely what *Baseball: The Sports Playbook* deals with.

A fine player need not necessarily have a combination of super speed, quickness, agility, and strength. Baseball is a highly strategic game. Knowing *what* to do in a particular situation is every bit as important as knowing *how* to do it. Knowing what to do and where to be during the play will make you a much better player—as well as allowing you to compensate for any skill you may lack. Baseball, more than any other sport, can be "learned," and from this learning process comes a marked increase in level of performance—an increase that is not subject to the limitations of physical capability.

Major league managers differentiate between errors of commission and those of omission. The former are mechanical miscues any human being will occasionally commit on the ball field, while the latter are mental mistakes which don't show up in the boxscore but contribute to a loss just as surely. This *Sports Playbook* contains all the information needed to help you prevent such errors. It alerts the reader to whatever situations he is likely to face in the course of a game and explains how to anticipate them, recognize them, and react correctly to them. This aspect of the game, as much as any other, is the reason baseball is fun to play, and the reason why this book can help any player who has ever taken the field or stepped into a batter's box.

In baseball, as in most other team sports, defense is the key. Through the years, the best defensive teams have won the highest share of championships, so defense is stressed here.

An expression golfers use when putting applies to the upcoming pages of this book. On the green, the player farthest from the cup putts first. Any golfer whose ball is closer to the cup but on the same line with it marks the spot and picks up his ball. He has a significant advantage; he can watch the break of the other golfer's ball, read the speed of the green and its contours; he can, the saying goes, "go to school" on the first player's putt. You, too, can "go to school" on this book.

The hundreds of examples covered in it will tell you what is expected of you, no matter what position you play, and what is expected of every other player on the field. Trial and error—a wasteful system at best—is eliminated. After reading *Baseball: The Sports Playbook,* no matter what situation you face on the diamond, you have been there before.

BASEBALL:

The Sports Playbook

GENERAL INFIELD PLAY

The inner defense—first base, second base, shortstop, and third base—is the most vital part of a team. More games are decided by good or poor play in the infield than anywhere else.

1.

There are certain physical things you look for in an infielder—the ability to field ground balls, the ability to throw from different body positions plus sure hands, quick reactions, and agility. These last three are all natural talents, but the other two attributes can be learned.

Learning to field grounders can be a tedious process, but only through

2. Proper position when fielding a grounder.

3. Watching the ball right into the glove.

4. Body and especially hands are kept in readiness.

constant practice can picking up a ground ball become second nature. The really good infielders have a coach hit them hundreds of ground balls daily.

The most important thing in fielding a grounder is to get in front of the ball and not turn your head (Illustration 2). If you watch the ball all the way, you have less chance of missing it (Illustration 3). It is also dangerous to shy away from a ball. If a ball takes a bad hop and you have taken your eye off it, it could hit you in the head and cause a serious injury. But if you are watching the ball all the way and it takes a bad hop, you'll find that your natural reflexes will protect you from getting hit.

In fielding grounders it is necessary to stay very low, especially with your hands. Bend your knees and keep your butt close to the ground (Illustration 4). You'll find that if your body is down low, you will be able to come up quickly, but that if your body is straight up it will be difficult to get down.

Always move toward the ball. By so doing you not only save time but are able to get in front of the ball properly and increase your chances of getting a good hop. You should always strive to field a ball on the big hop or the short hop since it is easier to handle in either of these two positions. The most difficult to field is the half-hop, which is midway between the ball's just coming off the ground and the peak of the hop.

The key to being a good infielder is anticipation. You should always expect the ball to be hit to you, and you should know precisely what to do with it when you field it. Therefore, you must have knowledge of the game situation, the speed of the opposing base runners, the abilities of the opposing batters, the types of pitches your pitcher throws, and the conditions of the playing field.

Knowing the speed of the base runners helps you in positioning yourself in the infield. A fast runner increases the possibility of a bunt or a steal, and it would be to your advantage to adjust your defense accordingly.

If you don't see a player perform too often, the best way to get a rundown on his ability is to get out to the park early and watch the other team take outfield and infield practice. You can usually spot the speed of a player during these drills.

In pro ball you have a much better knowledge of the hitters than you do in college or high school. But you can get a general idea of a hitter's style if you watch him take batting practice. You can generally tell from batting practice whether a batter hits straightaway or pulls the ball.

It is important for an infielder to know what pitch the pitcher is throwing. If there is a pull-hitter at bat and your pitcher is throwing him a breaking ball, chances are good that the batter will be pulling it even more. Thus, you can shade a little more in the direction where you expect him to hit it.

Knowing the condition of the playing field, including the position of the sun and the direction of the wind, is vital to an infielder. If you don't know the condition of the field you don't know how the ball is going to be reaching you. Certain fields are slow; others are extremely fast.

It's important to test the dirt in the infield prior to the start of the game. You might find, if you're playing shortstop, for example, that the composition of the soil is such that when you go into the hole to your right you

5. Running a base runner down correctly.

might dig in six inches when you put on the brakes. If you're not aware of this, it might throw you off balance and cause you to make a bad throw.

A common practice on home fields of teams that are not very quick defensively is for the ground crew to wet down the area considerably around home plate. This makes it difficult to drive the ball through the infield. If you have a good quick infield, however, the manager usually wants to keep the playing surface dry since his team will be able to field most of the grounders, and when batting will have a better chance of hitting the ball through for a base hit.

You should always make it a practice to find out which way the wind is blowing. Remember, the wind often changes direction during the course of a game so spot checks are necessary. The easiest way to check is to pick up some grass, flip it in the air, and see which way it carries. The wind can play havoc with a ball, and if you aren't aware of sudden changes in wind direction, you can make a careless mistake that could cost your team a game.

The sun is also the cause of many problems in fielding, and it is a good

6. Proper positioning on a steal attempt.

idea for both infielders and outfielders to wear sun glasses at all times. Wear the glasses even during practice so that you become used to them. Certain areas in certain parks are always "sun" fields—i.e., left field in Yankee Stadium and right field in Fenway Park—and an infielder chasing a ball into the sun should try to field it at an angle to cut down the glare.

There are two situations involving general infield play that are often troublesome to young players and a constant source of irritation to a coach or manager. These are the rundown play and the steal.

The rundown play, which occurs anytime you have a runner caught between two bases, quite often results in a missed putout among inexperienced infielders. The key to making the putout is for the man who has the ball to run the base runner as hard as he can back to the base he came from. NEVER force the runner toward the next base. Also, try to make only one throw. The fewer times the ball changes hands, the less chance there is for an error. Run at the base runner with the ball extended over your head, so when you get ready to throw you just flick the ball to the infielder covering the base (Illustration 5).

Once you get rid of the ball you must avoid colliding with the runner or you will be called for interference. If you don't have the ball, the base path belongs to the runner.

The steal play causes problems because many young players do not know how to make the tag correctly and, as a result, are often spiked or injured in a collision. In making the tag properly, the base should be used as a protective device. When you see the runner start to break, run as fast as you can to the base you're covering and straddle the bag in such a way that your feet are slightly in front of the base (Illustration 6). Catch the ball with the gloved hand and bring it down in a sweeping motion in front of the base as the man is sliding in. That way, the runner should literally be tagging himself out. The sweeping tag is used to prevent the runner from jarring the ball loose from your glove and to avoid injuries. Never leave your gloved hand in a stationary position in front of the bag.

FIRST BASE

First base is perhaps the easiest position to play in the infield because speed and a good throwing arm aren't that important. The things a manager or coach looks for most in a first baseman are good hands and the ability to shift his body well. Catching thrown balls is the first baseman's basic job, and you want a man at that position who can handle any type of thrown ball.

It is helpful if a first baseman is tall. A tall man can offer a better target and can stretch out much farther to catch throws, thereby cutting down the distance between himself and the person throwing the ball. The ability to stretch well can often save a half-step on the base runner.

First base is a good position for a left-hander because a left-hander has more natural advantages. For one thing, most of the throws a first baseman makes are to his right. Such a throw is simple for a left-hander, whereas a right-hander must pivot his body and shift his feet to make the same throw.

Secondly, a left-hander wears his glove on his right hand—which enables him to field more ground balls to his right than a right-hander could.

Where a first baseman positions himself under normal conditions depends on his agility. Some quick ones will play as far as 12 feet off the base; others must stay closer to the foul line. Where you play should be determined by the type of hitter at the plate—you'll play closer to the line for a left-handed pull-hitter than you will for a batter who hits to center and left, for instance —and how long it takes you to get back to first in order to receive a thrown ball.

If you're playing 12 feet off the base but find you're not fast enough to get over to first to receive a throw from an infielder, then you've been playing out of position. There is never any excuse not to be at the base when the infielder is ready to throw. You never want an infielder throwing to a running target or an empty base. A safe position to play would be about 15 feet behind the base and 8 feet off it.

One of the tougher plays for a first baseman occurs on a ball hit into the hole between first and second. Some first basemen will wander far to their

7.

right to get such balls, leaving first base uncovered. That is all right only if the pitcher covers first base. Otherwise, it is best to let the second baseman handle such plays—providing you know where he has positioned himself before the ball is hit.

In holding a runner on base, the first baseman should position himself

8. *First baseman's position when holding a runner on.*

with his right foot leaning against the inner edge of the bag and his left foot near the foul line (Illustration 8). It is important not to get your right foot out any farther than the edge of the bag. Otherwise, you might get spiked when a runner comes back into the base.

When a pick-off attempt from the pitcher is made to first, the first baseman should take the throw and in one sweeping motion lay the ball down with his gloved hand in front of the base. This play is harder for a right-hander, since he must bring his arm across his body to make the tag. On a pick-off attempt from the catcher, the first baseman must also remember to make his body pivot and tag in one sweeping motion (Illustration 9).

Whenever the first baseman thinks a runner is taking too big a lead, he can flash a pitchout sign to the catcher, or vice versa. In either case, it is important for the first baseman not to move too early so as to give the play away. The pick-off sign can be flashed no matter where the first baseman is playing, and it is the first baseman's responsibility to get to the base as quickly as he can. When this play works, which is seldom, it is usually only the good base runners who get caught. This play won't work against the runners who refuse to take a big lead.

The first baseman will not always hold a runner on first. There are times when he will play about 10 feet behind the runner, but this will depend on the score of the game, how many runners are on base and who those base runners are.

For example, when the defending team has a big lead and there is little

9. First baseman's position on a pick-off throw from the catcher.

10. First baseman's position on infield throws.

chance of a steal, there is no reason for the first baseman to hold the runner on. Or if there is an extremely slow runner on first it is usually better for the first baseman to position himself at normal depth behind the bag so that he is in a better spot to field anything hit his way. With runners on first and second and two outs, it is also better to play behind the runner.

Late in the game, when you want to guard against an extra-base hit, the first baseman should move a few steps closer to the line. Most first basemen play about 5 feet off the line in this situation, but again it depends on the player's agility.

The bunt play is one of the hardest plays for a first baseman to make. If there is a runner on first or runners on first and second and a bunt is anticipated, the first baseman should charge toward the plate as soon as the pitcher starts his delivery. The key to cutting off the lead runner is getting in there quickly and fielding the ball cleanly. The catcher will instruct you on whether to throw to second or third, but if he says nothing it means that your only throw is to first base.

With runners on first and second and a bunt anticipated, the first baseman should "cheat" a little by playing in on the edge of the infield grass. The big play, of course, is to get that force at third, but this is a maneuver that is extremely difficult for a first baseman to make. To make it successfully, he must field the ball and throw it all in one motion, and the pitcher must keep the runner on second close to the base. (This is a good time to try a pick-off play.)

In order to play first base well, you must be able to shift to either side of the base to catch thrown balls. If the first baseman uses the base as his pivot point, he'll find that he can go either way rather easily.

It is best to anchor the heels of both feet up against the base, so that you are in a position to shift to either side (Illustration 10). If the throw is to the right, you can shift to the right and tag the base with your left foot. If the throw is to the left, the opposite would apply. Sometimes, a throw will be down the first base line and in the path of the runner. Then the first baseman must catch the ball and put a sweeping tag on the runner.

If a throw is high, a first baseman should use the extra height provided by the bag. Low throws should be handled with the palm of the glove facing upward.

One of the most difficult things to teach a first baseman is when to stretch for a thrown ball. Most don't realize when they should be stretching for a ball and when they should be laying back. Some tend to overextend themselves stretching, while others don't stretch at all.

When to stretch must be determined by the speed of the runner and the speed of the throw coming over. A first baseman must determine in a split second whether or not to stretch. You should never commit yourself on a stretch until you see where that ball is going to be. Once you stretch out for a throw you're in a locked position and it is impossible to right yourself in time to catch a throw that is off line.

There are times when a first baseman fields a grounder and is unable to

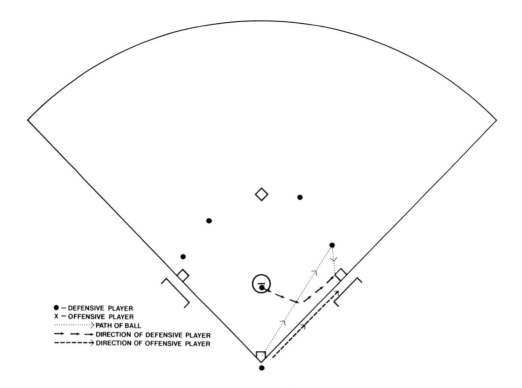

11. Pitcher's route on a grounder hit wide of first.

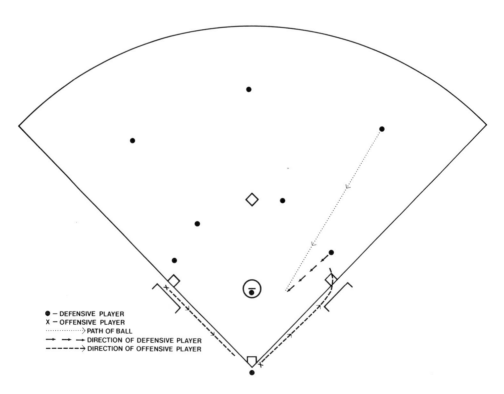

12. First baseman's position on a throw home from right field.

beat the runner to first base to make the putout. On such occasions he depends on the pitcher to cover the base. When the first baseman fields the ball, the pitcher should break toward the base line, make almost a 90-degree angle, turn, and run parallel to the line toward first base (Illustration 11). The first baseman, if he is close to the pitcher, will deliver a soft throw (underhand if possible) toward the base that the pitcher can catch on the run while crossing the bag. It is important that the first baseman keep the throw between the letters and the waist so that the pitcher can handle it easily.

This play is one of the more difficult to make and requires much practice to perfect.

The first baseman serves as a cut-off man on throws to the plate from right or center field. On throws from right field, he should position himself between the first-base line and pitcher's mound in a direct line between the catcher and the right fielder (Illustration 12). On a throw from center, a lot of first basemen will take the throw on the pitcher's mound in order to guard against the ball taking a bad hop if it should happen to hit the mound (Illustration 13).

On all cut-offs, the catcher directs the action. If he yells to cut the ball off, the first baseman should try to nail the runner at second. If he says nothing, let the throw go through to the plate.

One thing that separates a good first baseman from an average one is his ability to make the 3-6-3 double play. This is a much easier play for a left-hander since he does not have to turn toward second to make the throw; he can, instead, throw across his body. A right-hander must turn toward his right and face second before making the throw, and this can waste valuable seconds.

A right-hander must remember ALWAYS to pivot toward the infield when making the throw to second. That is, he must turn so that his left foot is extended toward second when he makes the throw. He should NEVER turn toward his left and spin completely around. That not only takes longer, but it inevitably forces the first baseman to take his eyes off second base, thus increasing the chances for a wild throw.

Once the throw has been made to second, the first baseman must run as fast as he can back to first base to await the return throw. Sometimes, the first baseman is so far off the base when he makes the throw that it is impossible for him to get back to the bag in time. Then it is the pitcher's responsibility to cover first.

The first baseman should be very active in handling pop flies, since he generally has good hands and a big glove. It is not a first baseman's responsibility to handle pop flies down the line, although he should join in the pursuit just in case the wind might blow it back toward the infield. The foul ball down the line is a far easier play for the second baseman since he has a better angle of approach.

The first baseman should, however, catch all pop-ups in the area from first base into home plate and those around the left side of the pitcher's mound. It is far easier for him to handle such pop flies than either the catcher or the

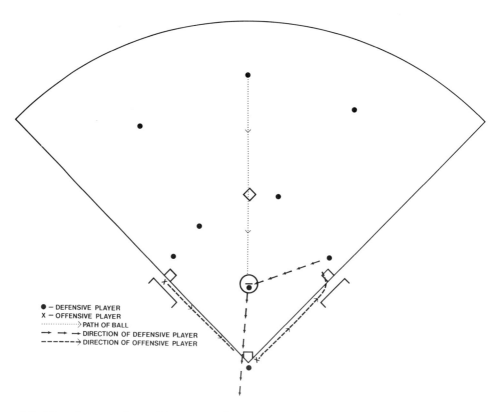

13. First baseman's position on a throw home from center field.

pitcher, and as soon as the ball is in the air the first baseman should call for it.

On topped balls in front of the plate, the first baseman must provide a target for the catcher by extending his glove within fair territory. The throw will hit the runner unless it is made to the inside of the base. The runner must run within the designated 3-foot line toward the outside of the foul line in the last half of the distance toward first. If he runs inside the 3-foot line, and in so doing interferes with the throw to first, he will be declared out.

SECOND BASE

The most important quality a second baseman can have is quickness. A strong arm is not essential because the throws a second baseman has to make are relatively short, and if you position yourself properly speed is not important. Quickness—the ability to get to the bag and get rid of the ball

fast—is the key to making the double play or the force play, which is the most important function of a second baseman.

Knowing where a batter hits the ball and how fast he runs determines where a second baseman normally plays. If there is no one on base, the second baseman will play shallow or deep depending on the batter's running speed. If there is a runner on first base, however, the second baseman's position in the field must be determined by the runner's known quickness. A second baseman should never be so far from second that he will not be at the bag waiting for a throw no matter how hard the ball is hit to one of the other infielders.

For example, if there is a runner on first and a right-handed pull-hitter at the plate, you shouldn't be more than 8 steps off second base. If you get farther away than that, you're asking for trouble. You might find yourself not getting to the bag quickly enough and that's when all the problems arise.

The second baseman's job is hardest when there is a runner on first and less than two out. He must be alert to the possibility of a steal, bunt, hit-and-run, or double play, and he is the key man in all of these situations.

With a runner on first and less than two out, it is probably best for the second baseman to move in a few steps from his normal position toward the pitcher. Now he is still in a position to field a grounder, but he has reduced the distance he will have to run to either first or second.

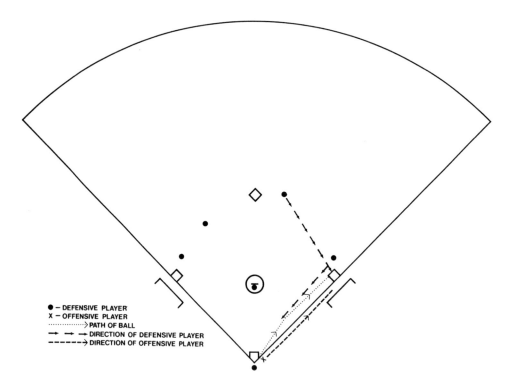

● – DEFENSIVE PLAYER
X – OFFENSIVE PLAYER
·············> PATH OF BALL
→ → → DIRECTION OF DEFENSIVE PLAYER
------→ DIRECTION OF OFFENSIVE PLAYER

15. Second baseman's responsibility on a bunt attempt.

On a bunt, it is the second baseman's responsibility to cover first base as the first baseman will be charging the plate (Illustration 15). In the event the first baseman can get back to cover the base, the second baseman will back up first base.

In a bunt situation, it is important that the second baseman not move before the action occurs at the plate. If the ball hasn't reached the batter and you're moving beforehand, an experienced hitter might try a hit-and-run. If he catches you leaning the other way, he may try to hit it at you and your movement could be the difference in fielding the ball or not fielding it.

The big play for the second baseman, as mentioned before, is the double play. Second basemen who have trouble making the double play are essen-

16. Second baseman's pivot (inside throw) on the double play.

17. Second baseman's pivot (outside throw) on the double play.

tially bothered by one of three things—faulty footwork, poor body control, or fear of getting hit by the base runner.

The best way of helping players get over the problem of poor footwork is to teach them to straddle the bag. This gives them the feel of the bag under their feet, and from that position they can easily learn to execute the double play.

Body control can best be learned by teaching the second baseman to slow down as he approaches the base. As soon as the ball is hit, the second baseman should break as fast as he can toward second. But when he is about 2 or 3 yards from the bag he should slacken his speed and get his body under control. Body control is important in making the correct pivots to complete the double play.

There are several pivots a second baseman can use, and the one he selects will largely depend on where the ball is caught.

If the ball is thrown toward the second baseman's left, or inside the base, the easiest method to use is to step toward the throw with your left foot. Drag your right foot across the bag and throw (Illustration 16). If the throw is to your right side, drag your left foot over the bag. You will then be able to anchor your right foot and throw (Illustration 17).

The easiest method of all is to throw precisely from where you catch the ball, simply by straddling the bag with your right foot leaning against the base.

Try not to use the same pivot all the time. An intelligent base runner will go out of his way to dump the second baseman if he sees that he makes the pivot the same way every time.

There is really no excuse for a second baseman to be hit by an incoming runner. If you're hit, you haven't judged the speed of the runner correctly or you were late getting to the base. Practice getting rid of the ball faster and you can avoid the possibility of collisions.

An important thing to remember when attempting a double play is not to throw the ball to first unless you are sure you have a good chance of retiring the batter. A teammate can help considerably in this situation by hollering "no play" if he sees that there is no chance of nailing the runner at first.

When the second baseman starts the double play he should, if possible, maneuver his body so that he can field the ball on his throwing side. Then he pivots his hips and throws at the shortstop's chest. A normal throw is used in most cases. But if you are within 3 or 4 feet of second base when you field the ball, you should give the shortstop an underhand toss so that the throw will be easy to handle.

There are times when the second baseman can tag the runner between first and second, then throw to first to complete the double play. If the runner stops before he gets to you, throw the ball to first for the putout, and

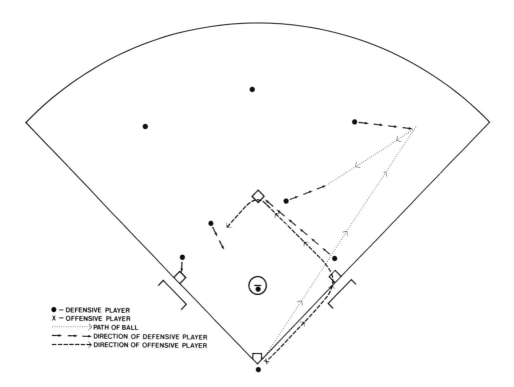

18. Second baseman's responsibility on an extra-base hit to right field.

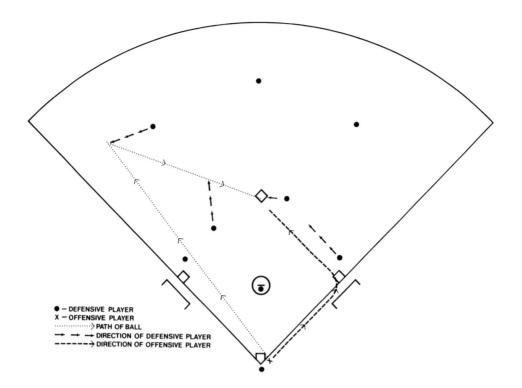

19. Second baseman's responsibility on an extra-base hit to left field.

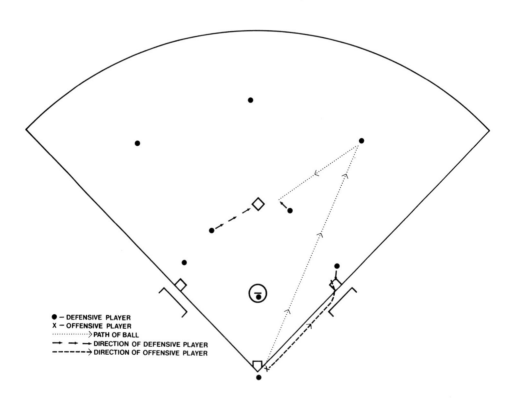

20. Second baseman's responsibility on a single to right, bases empty.

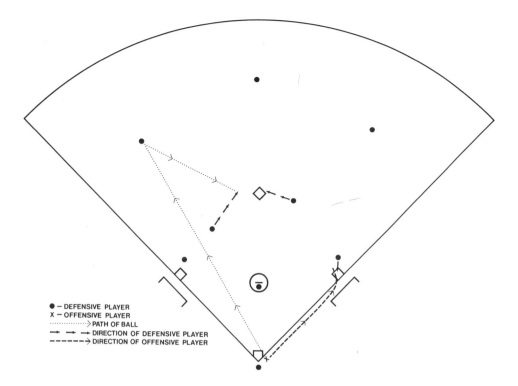

21. Second baseman's responsibility on a single to left, bases empty.

you will then have the runner going to second caught in a rundown. If the runner going to second runs out of the base line, don't follow him. He will be called out automatically, and you should complete your throw to first.

The double play is one of the most difficult plays in baseball, but one of the most vital. Practice constantly with your shortstop and get to know each other's moves so that the play will become second nature to you.

While a second baseman doesn't need as much range as a shortstop, he is responsible for quite an area on pop flies. A second baseman should take any shallow-hit ball to right field or down the right-field line, unless he is called off the play by the right fielder. Once he hears the outfielder holler for it, the second baseman should get out of the way as quickly as he can to avoid a collision.

Pop flies hit down the right-field line in foul territory are easier for a second baseman to handle than a first baseman, since the second baseman is approaching the ball from an angle.

On an extra-base hit to right field, the second baseman acts as the relay man and must hustle into short right field and line himself up with the right fielder and third base (Illustration 18). On an extra-base hit to left field, the second baseman's responsibility is to cover second (Illustration 19).

On a single to right field with no one on base, the second baseman should be the cut-off man with the shortstop covering second base (Illustration 20). On a hit to left, the situation is reversed (Illustration 21).

If the single is to center field, the player who did not attempt to field the ball should cover second with the other acting as cut-off man. If both players made an attempt to field the ball, then the one closest the base should take the throw-in.

SHORTSTOP

The shortstop must have the most poise of any player on the field except the catcher. He must be quick, have an extremely good arm, and a fine pair of hands.

A good shortstop can be judged in two ways: 1) how he reacts when the game is close, and 2) how well he makes the double play. You want a player at shortstop who doesn't get flustered when his team is one run ahead and the opposition has the bases loaded and only one out.

The shortstop must have the surest pair of hands of any of the infielders. He must field every ground ball cleanly in order to have a chance of throwing out the runner, since the throw he has to make is a fairly long one.

The key to being an outstanding shortstop is being able to field the ball and throw from where you catch it. A shortstop has many difficult throws to make, and the more adept he becomes at throwing the ball from the position in which he fields it, the better shortstop he will become.

An example of "throwing the ball from where you catch it" would be the slow-hit ball past the pitcher's mound. A quick, off-balance throw is necessary in this case, and it must be made from down low (where you've fielded the ball) in order to have a chance of getting the runner.

The same goes for the play deep in the hole near third. There is no time to straighten up and throw. You must anchor that right foot and let loose with a strong, accurate throw from whatever position you have fielded the ball.

Where a shortstop positions himself under normal circumstances depends a great deal on the strength of his arm and his range. Some shortstops with very strong arms can afford to shade a little deeper toward the outfield and still have no trouble throwing the runner out at first.

There are limits to a good arm, however, and you must remember that all diamonds aren't cut the same way. Some diamonds are cut very deep, and what looks like a routine throw is really abnormal. You've got to find the spot out there where you know you can throw the man out. Also, your position in the field must allow you to make both the play in the hole and the play over second base.

22.

Of all the infielders, it is most important for the shortstop to learn to "play the ball" and not have the ball play him. That means he must learn to charge grounders so that he gets the good hop on most occasions.

When there is a runner on first base and less than two out, a shortstop should move a little closer to second base to get ready for a possible double play. The only time he would not shade a bit toward second is if there is a right-handed pull-hitter up. In that situation, the shortstop would move a few steps in the opposite direction toward third base.

When starting the double play, it is important that the shortstop give the second baseman a throw he can handle easily. Most second basemen prefer the ball to be thrown toward a certain spot—either inside or outside or directly at the base—and the second baseman should inform the shortstop of his preference.

The shortstop should try at all times to feed the ball to the second baseman with his bare hand, so that the second baseman doesn't lose sight of it. Many experienced shortstops will flip the ball to the second baseman with their gloved hand if they are close enough to the base, but this practice should be discouraged. While it may save a second in getting rid of the ball, it is not recommended since quite often the second baseman loses sight of the ball and may drop the throw.

23. *Shortstop's pivot (outside throw) on the double play.*

24. Shortstop's pivot (direct or inside throw) on the double play.

As in the case of the second baseman, there is no excuse for the shortstop not to make it to the base in time to start the double play. He must position himself in such a way that he can make it to second base in time no matter how hard or where that ball is hit.

There is no specific way for the shortstop to make the pivot on the double play. Most shortstops like the ball thrown to the outside of the base, so they can drag their right foot across the bag and be going toward first base when they throw (Illustration 23). However, it is better if you can train the second baseman to throw the ball right at the bag or to the inside, since this way it is easier to avoid the base runner (Illustration 24). Also, your pivot in this instance would carry you toward first base rather than right field.

There is absolutely no excuse for a shortstop to be taken out of a play by a sliding base runner. At shortstop, the play is always in front of you and there are numerous ways of avoiding the runner. Any time you are decked by a sliding runner the chance of injury is great, and no team can afford to lose its shortstop for any length of time.

One of the important functions of a shortstop is giving signals to the other infielders. In a steal situation, it is the shortstop's job to signal the second baseman as to who will cover second. This is done by the use of "open and closed" mouth signs.

The shortstop holds his glove up to his face, looks at the second baseman and either opens his mouth or closes it tight. Open mouth usually means the second baseman will cover and closed mouth indicates the shortstop will cover. Generally, the shortstop will cover second when there is a left-handed batter at the plate and the second baseman will cover against right-handed batters.

The shortstop, since he is in perfect position to see the catcher's signs to the pitcher, may also give a word sign to the third baseman if an off-speed pitch is on its way which the batter might hit toward the third baseman's area. Any word can be used.

The shortstop must use his voice quite often in directing traffic on the field. He should be the one who tells the other infielders where they should throw the ball in a given situation, and he should also call out who is to catch a pop fly in case of doubt between two players.

In regular bunt situations, it is the shortstop's job to cover second. With a runner on second and the possibility of a bunt, it is the shortstop's job to keep that runner close to second. This can be done by working a pick-off play with the pitcher.

The pick-off play at second can be a dangerous play unless executed properly. It requires precise timing on the part of both the pitcher and the shortstop. A prearranged signal is given by the pitcher to inform the shortstop that he will try a pick-off play.

Prior to working the pick-off play, the shortstop can fake cutting in behind the runner a couple of times. This may keep the runner close to second, but even if it doesn't, it gives the shortstop a chance to slowly inch closer to second. Each time the shortstop backs off from his fake attempt, he gives the illusion of returning to his normal position by moving backward a few steps. But at the same time he should be inching closer to second.

The pitcher may inform the shortstop that he is going to try a pick-off play by tossing the resin bag in the direction of second base just before he gets in a set position on the pitching rubber. As soon as the pitcher gets set, both he and the shortstop begin counting to three.

In order not to give the play away, the shortstop should break for second on the count of two. Then, at three, the pitcher wheels toward his glove side and fires to second. Needless to say, the shortstop must be there or you'll end up with a runner on third. The center fielder is responsible for backing up on this play.

A shortstop's range is put to the test most often on pop flies to the outfield. The shortstop should try to catch any pop fly to left or center field he can get to, unless he is called off by the outfielder. On pop flies down the left field line, the shortstop has a much better angle on the ball than the third baseman and should assume the responsibility for catching it.

In going after pop flies, use the crossover step and run as fast as you can until you have positioned yourself under the ball. Do not backpedal on pop flies unless they are very high and only a few feet behind you on the edge of the outfield grass.

The shortstop also has a major responsbility in backing up bases on attempted steals. He backs up second and third on attempted steals, and also backs up the pitcher with runners on base when the pitcher is forced to cover home on a wild pitch or passed ball.

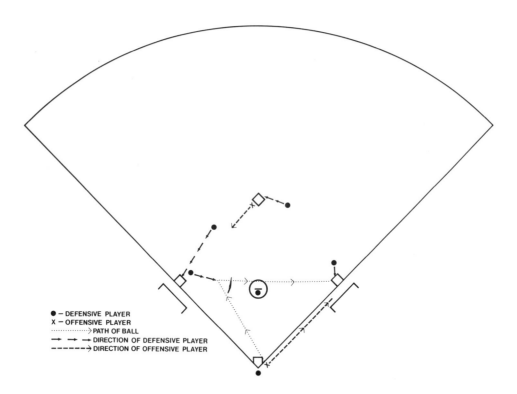

25. Shortstop's responsibility on slow-hit ball to third, runner on second.

The shortstop also has a responsibility to cover third when there is a runner on second and the third baseman has fielded a slow-hit ball in the hole (Illustration 25). In most cases the third baseman will be unable to retreat to the bag on this play, so he must "look" the runner back to second before throwing to first for the out. The shortstop must cover third to further assure that the runner on second won't be able to advance.

The shortstop acts as a relay man on extra-base hits to left field and center field. Occasionally, on an extra-base hit to right field, the shortstop may also act as relay man instead of the second baseman because of his stronger throwing arm.

THIRD BASE

Physical strength and a strong throwing arm are the two most important attributes of a third baseman. He must be physically strong so that he can block hard-hit balls with his body, if necessary, and he must have a strong, accurate arm since it is a fairly long throw across the diamond.

Where the third baseman plays depends on several factors. He must take into consideration the type of batter at the plate, his running speed, where he usually hits the ball, whether he bunts or not, and, of course, the game situation.

The normal third-baseman's position for a batter who does not bunt is approximately 10 to 15 feet from the foul line and about 2 or 3 yards behind the base. If the batter is a "pull-hitter," the third baseman should move slightly closer to the line.

The size of the individual is a determining factor in what stance to take in the field. A small man would have his feet closer together than a taller man, but you should always guard against having your stance too wide. If your stance is too wide, it will slow you down in making that first movement toward the ball. You should be going at full speed on the first step.

It is important to stay very low, especially with your hands. Bend your knees and get your butt close to the ground. You'll find that if you're down low you can come up quickly, but if you're standing up your body just won't get down as fast. Keep your body in front of every ground ball and expect a bad hop on every play. If you do, you'll find that fielding is not as hard as it appears.

One of the advantages of playing third base is that you don't have to field the ball cleanly on every play to make the putout. On hard-hit balls, it is only necessary to knock the ball down with your body. You still have plenty of time to pick it up and throw out the runner.

If a team is ahead by a run going into the eighth or ninth inning, most managers and coaches prefer their third baseman to play a little closer to the foul line in order to guard against an extra-base hit. But it is not a good idea for a third baseman to play close to the line consistently. Many more balls

26.

are hit into the area between shortstop and third base than are hit down the line. If a third baseman is playing off the base by 10 or 15 feet, he is therefore in a better position to field most ground balls.

A third baseman who plays well off the line is a tremendous help to the shortstop. The shortstop can then afford to shade a little toward second base, which enables him to reach balls hit up the middle.

The toughest play for a third baseman is fielding a bunt. The main thing in fielding bunts is anticipating the play and getting to the ball quickly. You should always be alert to the possibility of a bunt whenever the score is close and there is a runner on first and/or second with less than two out.

Watch the batter's hands! Sometimes, he'll give the bunt away by moving his hands up the bat as the pitcher begins to throw. Some players even shift their feet and face the pitcher as the ball is thrown. If this happens, the third baseman should be well up toward the batter waiting for the bunt.

DO NOT field a bunt bare-handed. Many professional players like to make the play that way (Brooks Robinson of the Baltimore Orioles probably makes it better than anyone), but the percentage is against you. It's very difficult to get a good grip on the ball fielding it one-handed. It is much better to field the ball with the glove, holding your hands close together, and then throwing the ball crisply to first base.

There's nothing more embarrassing than to see a third baseman make what looks like a great bare-handed play, then throw the ball into the stands. He would have been better off if he let the ball roll down the line and allowed the runner to reach first base.

Bunts and slow-hit balls should be fielded the same way. Any ball that's moving should be fielded with the glove. Once in a while, a ball will have a lot of underspin on it and just die when it hits the ground. In that situation, you could make the play bare-handed since it is a "do or die" thing. However, your chances of getting the man out are very slim.

A third baseman should make an attempt to field all slow-hit balls to his left, as it is doubtful that the shortstop can get to the ball from his deep position in time to retire the batter. Nevertheless, if the ball is hit moderately slow and the shortstop calls out, "I've got it," the third baseman lets him make the play.

The most important thing to remember when starting the double play from third is to try not to knock the second baseman off the bag. You must understand that the second baseman has to make his pivot and throw quickly in order to complete the double play. In order for him to execute properly, he must be able to handle your throw.

Get rid of the ball quickly, with good stuff on it, and throw it directly at the bag. If you do that, the second baseman will be able to execute his pivot

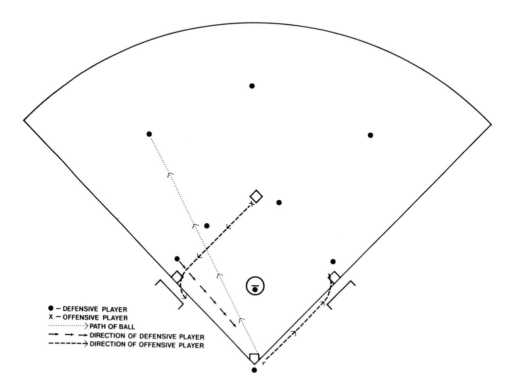

27. Third baseman's position on throw home from left field.

without taking any steps. He'll be throwing to first base right from where he catches your throw, which is the ideal way to make the play.

Don't waste time in getting rid of the ball. Field the ball, get rid of it quickly, and make an accurate throw to second base. The best throw is one that the second baseman can catch between his waist and letters.

There is no set way to throw the ball. Some players prefer to straighten up and throw overhand, while others throw the ball from where they field it. By throwing the ball from where you field it you can save time—and time is the main factor in completing a double play. It is best not to throw the ball sidearm, since a sidearm throw is not the easiest one to handle because it has a tendency to "sail."

With a runner on first, or runners on first and second and two out, the third baseman may elect to throw to second base for the force out. This is a smart move since it is a much shorter throw to second than to first. The exception in this situation would occur if the second baseman was playing the batter over near first base. In that event, the throw would be made to first.

The third baseman acts as the cut-off man when a single is hit to left field with a runner on second base (Illustration 27). The preferred spot to be in this situation is in a direct line with the left fielder and the catcher and about 25 feet from the catcher.

This might appear to be too close to the catcher, but in such a position you have a better chance of seeing out of the corner of your eye what the runner reaching first is going to do. Also, your communication with the catcher is better in this position. If you're only 20 feet or less off third base, you're in no position to see the runner rounding first and very often you won't be able to hear the catcher hollering to cut the ball off or let it go through to the plate.

The catcher will be silent if he thinks a play can be made at the plate on the runner from second. If he doesn't holler, the third baseman should fake catching the ball, thus preventing the runner or runners from taking the extra base.

If the left fielder's throw is off line, the catcher will holler "Cut," and the third baseman would then play the ball off his right shoulder since he can get rid of it quicker if he catches it on his throwing side. The fewer words exchanged between the two parties, the better.

On throws from center field and right field, the third baseman backs up second base unless he is involved in a play at third base. With first base unoccupied and a runner on second attempting to advance to third after "tagging up" on a fly ball, the third baseman covers third base while the shortstop becomes the cut-off man and the pitcher backs up third base (Illustration 28).

The tag play at third base is made no differently than at second. The only really tough tag play at third occurs when there's a left-handed batter at the plate and the third baseman is positioned farther to his left than normal. In this case, if a runner attempts to steal third, the third baseman has a longer run to get to the base. However, a steal attempt of third base with a left-

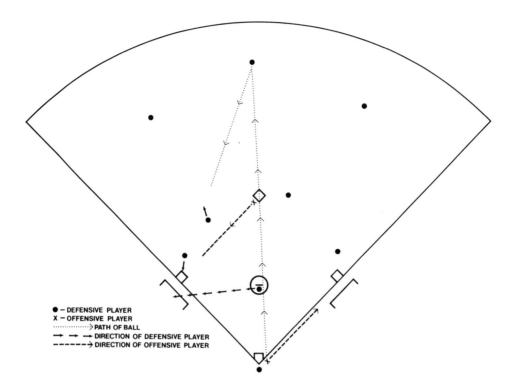

28. Third baseman's position on "tag-up" play at third.

handed batter up is not considered a good percentage play since the catcher has an easier throw to make.

There are times when the pitcher or catcher will attempt a pick-off play at third base, but this is done infrequently since one mistake on the part of either the pitcher, catcher, or third baseman could cost a run. A prearranged signal between the third baseman and the pitcher or catcher determines when a pick-off play is in order. One device that some pitchers use is to throw the resin bag in the direction of the base where the pick-off play is to be attempted.

CATCHER

Catcher is the most important position on the field. A catcher is like the director of a movie in that the action is always in front of him, and he is in the best position to control the flow of activity.

The three most important qualities for a catcher are good hands, a strong throwing arm, and quickness.

By good hands we mean the ability to handle every pitch—fast ball, curve, knuckler, slider, etc.—with relative ease. Passed balls can play a big part in the winning or losing of a game, and a catcher who is repeatedly dropping balls is a detriment to his team.

A catcher who can't throw well also hurts a team considerably. Everyone takes liberties on the base paths with a catcher who has a weak throwing arm. You want a man behind the plate who can throw a runner out when he has to.

Quickness, the ability to move well to either side, is perhaps a catcher's most important asset. Slow-moving catchers usually have difficulty handling the low and outside pitches. It is important that a catcher be able to shift quickly to either side and go down on his knees to block a ball if necessary.

A catcher's size isn't really important, although many managers or coaches prefer one who is relatively small in stature. A small catcher is able to give a lower target, which in turn, forces the pitcher to come down with his pitches. Once a pitcher throws high consistently, which he would have a tendency to do with a tall catcher, he is asking for trouble.

The catcher's job is to run the defense, and it is important for him to know as much or more about the opposing team's batters than the pitcher. Sometimes a pitcher has enough problems just putting the ball where he wants to, rather than spending time worrying about the hitter. So it becomes the catcher's responsibility to know every hitter's weakness and direct the pitcher accordingly.

A catcher plays an important part in helping a pitcher with his control problems. If the pitcher is throwing too high, the catcher can tell if he is releasing the ball too quickly. If he sees the pitcher's fast ball is not moving,

29.

he might detect that the pitcher is not throwing with his proper motion. In short, the catcher functions as a coach for the pitcher and is always alerting him to what he is doing wrong.

Two of the more important functions of a catcher, when working with the pitcher, are giving signs and providing a proper target.

The catcher and pitcher set up a series of signs between themselves before a game. Most of the time the finger method is used. That's where the catcher calls different pitches simply by showing a certain number of fingers on his bare hand to the pitcher. One finger extended might be a fast ball; two, a curve; three, a slider, etc.

It is important for the catcher to keep these signs easy for his infielders to see, yet at the same time keep them concealed from the other team.

With a runner on second, the signs would be given in a series so that the base runner could not detect them. In other words, the catcher might flash three signs to the pitcher—one-three-two or two-three-one—and the two players would have determined beforehand which of the three signs is to be used.

For night games, the finger method quite often is replaced by a "flap" method which is easier to detect under the lights. Here, the catcher uses his hand against the inner part of his leg as the basis for the signals. Thus the

30. Proper shifting position, catcher moving to his right.

31. Proper shifting position, catcher moving to his left.

hand resting against the leg might be the signal for a fast ball, and the hand flipped off the leg would be a curve.

In giving a target to the pitcher, it is important to get as low in the crouch as you can. Also, make sure that the glove is out over the plate in the area where you want the ball to be. Always have the glove down with the palm facing up when you go for a low ball.

Another important aspect of catching is shifting. A catcher must be able to·move quickly to either his left or his right without getting tangled up in his own footwork. The proper method of shifting can be learned rather easily, but the most important thing to remember is not to cross one foot over another. When shifting to your right, extend your right foot laterally and place your left foot slightly in front so that you are in a perfect throwing position (Illustration 30). When shifting to the left, move your left foot laterally and drop your right foot slightly behind to anchor yourself (Illustration 31). Now you're in a position to throw.

As mentioned before, one of the catcher's most vital assets is his hands, and he should always afford them the proper protection. Seldom does a season go by when a catcher doesn't injure his hands in some way. He handles so many breaking pitches and endures so many foul tips and home-plate collisions during the course of a season that an injury of some kind to his hands is almost inevitable. But there are some precautions you can take to help cut down on hand injuries.

For one thing, try not to keep your throwing hand clenched tight. If a ball is ticked and hits your throwing hand, the less resistance your hand offers the ball the better. Also, avoid moving forward to catch a pitch. Let the ball ride into you. It is also a good idea against exceptionally hard throwers to keep one or two fingers out of the glove to guard against bruises. Some catchers even wear a sponge to protect the palm of their hand from getting bruised by "heavy" balls.

We have mentioned the importance of a good throwing arm to a catcher, but a good arm by itself is not that valuable unless you have the quickness and alertness to know when to use it.

Anticipation is important to a catcher, especially in a steal situation. The good catchers can anticipate when a base runner may be stealing, and that is the time to call for a pitchout. The pitchout sign should be simple—such as wiggling the glove or flipping the thumb of your throwing hand—and it is important that the pitcher throw the pitch far enough outside so that the batter can't hit it and the catcher can handle it easily. A pitchout is often a good ploy to see if your opponents are bunting or hitting away.

On a steal of second, the catcher must rely heavily on his bench to tell him when the runner is going, especially if there is a left-handed batter at the plate and his vision toward first base is blocked. Of course, most runners steal on the pitcher and not the catcher, but the catcher's job can be made easier if the pitcher keeps the runner fairly close to first base by occasionally throwing over there.

It is not necessary to have an arm like Johnny Bench to throw a runner out at second. How quick you get rid of the ball is the key. If you reach way back to throw, the runner is going to have an advantage on you. It is better to come up to a position where your arm is at a right angle to your body and throw from off your ear (Illustration 32). Your weight should always be balanced on your rear, or right foot, and you should try to get a reverse spin on the ball so that it will carry better. Try to take only one step before releasing the ball. Too many steps before throwing wastes time and gives the runner a great advantage.

On a double-steal attempt with runners on first and third, the catcher has three alternatives. He can throw through to second base and have the short-

32. Catcher's position on snap throws to second base.

stop or second baseman either make the tag there or cut the ball off and try for the man at home. He can pretend he is throwing through to second and have the pitcher cut the ball off. Or he can make a bluff throw to second and quickly throw to third. It must be predetermined between the pitcher, short-stop, second baseman, and catcher how the play is to be worked.

The catcher's job as director of the infield comes into play the most in a bunt situation. Since the play is in front of the catcher and he can see the position of the base runners and all the other infielders, it is his assignment to call out who is to field the bunt and where he is to throw the ball.

It is better if the third baseman, first baseman, or pitcher can field the bunt, since they are coming in on the ball. However, if a catcher is forced to field a bunt, he should scoop up the ball with two hands, pivot toward the diamond, and fire the ball to first base. It is important that the catcher AL-WAYS pivot toward the diamond before making the throw to first. NEVER spin completely around and throw as it causes you to lose perspective of where first base is.

When it comes to handling pop-ups, a catcher is usually responsible for any foul ball inside an area diagonal from home plate to the beginning of each dugout, and any fair ball directly over the plate. Any time a ball is hit to the inside part of the diamond, the third or first baseman should handle it unless it is not hit very high. A soft pop-up in fair territory in the vicinity of home plate might be handled by the catcher or even the pitcher.

On pop-ups behind home plate, the catcher should field the ball away from his body, since the spin of the ball will carry it back toward fair territory. Pop flies in fair territory, or just over the catcher's head, will carry away from the catcher, and he should field the ball just off the top of his head.

One problem young catchers have in chasing after pop flies is getting rid of the mask. Many catchers who don't know how to discard the mask properly end up tripping over it, causing themselves serious injury or the embarrassment of having dropped the ball. It is best to hold onto the mask until you're at a point where you want to be, then discard it about 8 to 10 feet away from you. On windy days, throw the mask in the opposite direction from the way the wind is blowing.

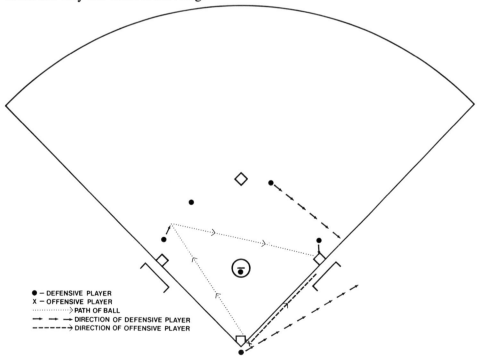

33. Catcher's responsibility on any infield grounder, bases empty.

The toughest of all plays for a catcher is blocking home plate against an incoming base runner. To block the plate effectively, you should be out in front of it up the third base line about 3 to 5 feet, and down on your knees with your body blocking the base path.

It is important not to take your eyes off the ball to watch the runner, and you should make the tag with the back of your glove holding the ball with two hands. Many young catchers have trouble with this play because they make the tag improperly. If you make the tag with both hands, there is less chance the ball will be knocked loose in a collision with the runner.

The rules stipulate that a catcher is allowed to block the plate only if he has possession of the ball. This rule is often loosely interpreted by umpires, however, and they will sometimes allow the catcher to block home plate if he is in the process of receiving the ball. But don't block the plate if you see there is going to be no play. Not only does it constitute interference, but it could lead to serious injury for both parties.

On all throws to the plate, the catcher decides whether or not the ball should be cut off. If the catcher yells "Cut," the cut-off man must throw to whatever base he can catch the runner. If the catcher remains silent, the ball should not be cut off as it means there is a play at home.

Another of the catcher's most important tasks is backing up or covering other bases. On any ground ball to the infield with no one on base, it is the catcher's responsibility to back up first base (Illustration 33). There are also times when he might cover third, such as in a rundown play. In that situation, it would be the first baseman's job to cover home.

As you can see, the catcher's job requires intelligence, durability, and leadership qualities. He is the important cog in the "up the middle" strength any team must have to be a winner.

PITCHER

Pitching, the experts say, is 90 per cent of baseball. And to be a good pitcher, one needs more than just the ability to blow the ball by the opposing batter.

A pitcher must possess all the fundamentals of an athlete—strength, agility, endurance, and mastery of skills—and he must also have the qualities of leadership such as courage, poise, and confidence since it is he who most often controls the outcome of a game.

A pitcher does not have to be big physically nor does he have to have an outstanding assortment of pitches to be superior at his trade. What he must be, however, is a student of the game and he must, above all, have control of his pitches.

If pitching is 90 per cent of baseball, then control is 90 per cent of pitching. Control doesn't just mean the ability to put the ball over the plate. Control means the ability to put the ball where you want it consistently so as to take advantage of a batter's weaknesses.

How does a pitcher learn control? The same way any athlete becomes good at his particular profession—by repetition. A pitcher must constantly work at his trade. A pitcher with control is like an expert dart thrower, with the catcher serving as the board and his glove serving as the bull's-eye.

Concentration is the key to good control. If you're aiming at a target, you're concentrating. Constant throwing is the only way to become efficient in mastering control. A young pitcher should throw constantly on the sidelines to a target. Pitching batting practice is no good. Batting practice is for the batter. Pitching practice should be done alone on the sidelines.

Controlling oneself is as important as learning to control one's pitches. Poise and self-control should be maintained at all times. The pitcher who gets disturbed over teammates' errors or his own wildness is only defeating himself. Pitching is an art that requires complete co-ordination of body and mind. An unsettled mind will cause you to lose your concentration and affect your physical actions.

We mentioned that a pitcher must be a student of the game to be success-

34.

ful. By this we mean he must have knowledge of the opposing hitters'
strengths and weaknesses, and he must know the effectiveness of his own
pitches, and what pitch to throw in certain situations.

All pitchers should make it a point to observe the opposing batters during
batting practice, even when they are not scheduled to pitch. You can get a
general idea of a batter's style if you watch him during batting practice. Is
he a free swinger? Does he overstride? Does he hit straightaway or is he an
opposite-field hitter? Make mental notes of the different batters' strengths
and weaknesses so that you can refer to them during a game.

A successful pitcher must have at least two pitches—preferably a fast ball
and curve—that he can control with regularity. By learning to change
speeds a pitcher can transform these two pitches into eight, and that's when he
is on his way toward becoming a winner. Changing speeds on pitches ruins the

timing of good hitters, and if you can change speeds on just two pitches you have an effective assortment. A pitcher, however, should always rely on his best pitch in a crucial situation.

No matter how many pitches a pitcher may have in his repertoire, the important thing is to learn to throw them all with the same motion. Often young and inexperienced pitchers will throw their curve ball with a different motion than their fast ball. This is a big advantage for the experienced batter, who will know in advance what pitch to expect.

If you throw your fast ball with a sidearm delivery, then you should learn to throw your curve sidearm. A good pitcher will also learn to grip every pitch the same way. Good hitters can detect the slightest adjustment of the pitcher's fingers and know that the adjustment means a certain pitch is on its way.

How a pitcher delivers the ball to home plate is a matter of individual preference. Some pitchers like to work from a big windup with no runners on base, others like the no-windup method. Either way is all right as long as the ball is concealed properly before it is delivered to the plate. Prior to winding up, the ball should be hidden behind the hip. Then as the pitcher brings his arm up to begin his delivery, the ball should be hidden behind the glove with the back of the glove facing the batter. With the ball concealed in this manner, the batter won't be able to see it until it is well on its way toward home plate.

With a runner on either first or second, or runners on both first and second, the pitcher works out of a set position. That means, if he is a left-hander, he is facing first base, or if he's a right-hander, his back is to first base. In the set position, the outer edge of the rear foot is barely touching the pitching rubber and the other foot is in front of the rubber in a position to maintain good balance (Illustration 35).

Proper balance is necessary to assure quick movement to either home plate or first base. Some pitchers put too much weight on the rear foot, thus preventing themselves from making a quick throw to first base. Others put too much weight on the front foot, which causes them to lose speed off their pitches.

One of the toughest plays for a right-handed pitcher is the pick-off attempt at first. A right-handed pitcher is at a disadvantage on this play since his back is to the base runner and it requires long hours of practice to perfect the play. It is important that pitchers develop an effective move toward first since it helps in keeping base runners from taking too big a lead. Remember, most base runners steal on the pitcher, NOT the catcher.

In developing a move toward first, it is very important to keep the left shoulder in as straight a line as possible toward home plate. Many pitchers make the mistake of moving their left shoulder too far to the left so they won't lose sight of the runner. But when they make their throw to first, the left shoulder is the first thing to move and the smart runner can take advantage of this and immediately break for second.

It is better to open your left leg a little more when you take your stance

35. Pitcher working out of the set position.

on the mound. By doing this, you can maintain a straight line toward home plate with your shoulder and still keep a close eye on the runner.

Be sure you don't make any movement toward home plate before throwing over to first, or that you don't fake a throw to first while standing on the pitching rubber. Both of those acts constitute a balk and the runner is allowed to move up a base.

There are about a dozen ways a pitcher can balk, and they are all the result of carelessness. If at any time you feel you might be on the verge of committing a balk, back off the rubber and the umpire will call time out. Incidentally, a pitcher can NEVER balk to second base. You can make as many fake throws as you want toward second while standing on the rubber without being penalized.

Holding a runner on first base is much easier for a left-hander, since he can literally "look" the runner back to the base. Most base runners take few liberties with left-handers, but don't assume that just because you're left-handed the runner won't try to steal on you.

Lou Brock, the great base-stealer of the St. Louis Cardinals, once said the easiest pitcher for him to steal against was Ken Holtzman, a left-hander. The reason was that Holtzman never even once threw to first base to keep Brock close. Brock learned this and realized he could take a big lead without worrying that Holtzman might pick him off.

So, while runners may be cautious against a left-hander, it's a good idea to throw over there once in awhile just to show them that you can.

Picking a runner off second is a far more difficult task than picking a runner off first, since there is no one at second holding the runner on base. The pick-off play at second is a precision play between the pitcher and shortstop and is described in the chapter on playing shortstop.

There is more to pitching than just throwing the ball to a batter. A pitcher is the fifth infielder, and he can help himself considerably if he learns to field his position properly.

A lot of pitchers think that fielding is not an integral part of pitching, but they're wrong. Many games are lost by poor fielding pitchers. All pitchers should try to get into pepper games during pregame warmups and get used to fielding balls hit to them. The only way a pitcher can start thinking like an infielder is to take a lot of grounders.

Like any other infielder, the pitcher should anticipate what to do with the ball if it is hit to him. On a ball hit back to the mound with runners on base, he must know beforehand where he is to throw the ball and who is going to take it. Normally, on a ball hit back to the pitcher with a runner on first, the shortstop will take the throw at second. But the shortstop should confer with the pitcher beforehand to make sure the pitcher knows who will be covering second.

The pitcher must be most alert in a bunt situation. He should be off the mound as soon as he releases the ball, ready to field any bunt in the area of the mound. Since second base is at his back, he must rely on the catcher to tell him where to throw the ball. It is important to field the ball cleanly and to make an accurate throw.

The bunt is an easier play for a right-handed pitcher, since he is facing first base when he fields the ball. The left-hander must make a 180-degree turn before throwing to first.

Another important function of the pitcher is to cover first base on all grounders hit toward the first baseman. A pitcher should get into the habit of breaking off the mound toward first on all balls hit to the left side of the infield.

The approach to first by the pitcher is made at a 90-degree angle, NOT on a diagonal from the pitcher's mound. The proper way to make the approach is to run in a straight line from the pitcher's mound to the first base line, then run along the first-base line to the bag. The first baseman must make a good lead throw and the pitcher should tag the base with his right

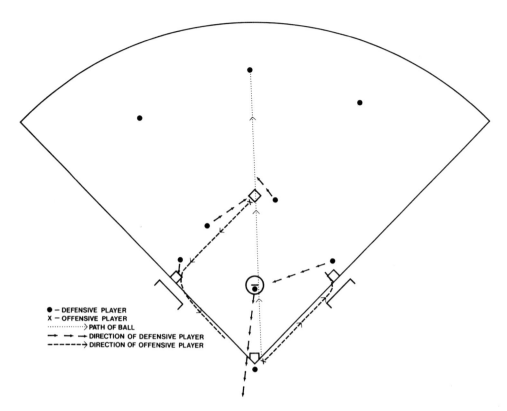

36. Pitcher's responsibility on an outfield hit, runner on second.

foot and step off to the left quickly so as to avoid a collision with the base runner.

By approaching first on a right angle from the pitcher's mound, you are giving the first baseman a better target and there is less chance of colliding with the runner. The only time you would approach first base on a diagonal line from the pitcher's mound is if you broke off the mound to field a bunt and it got by you. Then you would have to run directly to first.

A pitcher also has the responsibility of backing up bases. With a runner on first, the pitcher is responsible for backing up third on a single to the outfield. If there's a runner on second and a ball is hit safely to the outfield, the pitcher must back up home plate (Illustration 36). When there's an extra-base hit and a runner on first, the pitcher should go midway between third and home and back up the base where the play develops (Illustration 37). When backing up the base, don't stand too close to the action. The idea in backing up bases is to prevent the runners from taking an extra base in case the ball gets past the intended fielder. If you're too close to the play, a ball that eludes the man you're backing up is likely to get past you, too.

It is a pitcher's job to cover home plate on either a wild pitch or a passed

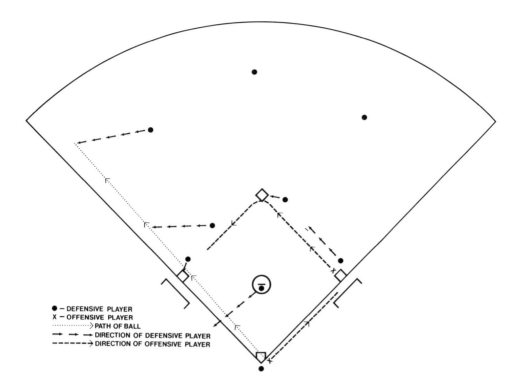

37. Pitcher's responsibility on an extra-base hit, runner on first.

ball with a runner on third. If you see the ball get away from the catcher, run for home plate as quickly as you can and get ready for a return throw from the catcher. Be prepared to make a tag play at the plate in the same way you would if you were playing an infield position.

As you can see, a pitcher's responsibility never ends. The pitcher who thinks his job is over as soon as he releases the ball to the plate is sadly mistaken. The pitcher who learns to field his position properly is a tremendous asset to a team and has taken a big step toward being a winning pitcher.

OUTFIELD

An outfielder should possess good running speed, sure hands, and a strong throwing arm, plus the ability to come in and retreat quickly.

The key man in the outfield is the center fielder, and he is usually the best defensively of the three. The right fielder normally has the strongest throwing arm because he has to make the longest throws, while the left fielder should have good speed but not necessarily a good arm since the throws he is required to make are relatively short.

To be a good outfielder you should know the ability of opposing batters and the speed of the base runners, and you must have knowledge of the playing conditions and the geographical features of the field.

Knowing a batter's strengths and weaknesses helps the outfielder in positioning himself properly. If there's a power-hitter at the plate, an outfielder would play deeper than he would for a singles hitter. If the batter is the type who goes to right field more than to left field, then the outfield should play him to hit to right. If the outfielder knows a particular batter can't pull a certain pitcher's fast ball, then he should play the batter to hit to the opposite field.

Knowing the speed of the base runners helps the outfielder determine how fast he must get to the ball if it is a base hit. If there's a single to left, for example, and you don't know the speed of the runner, you may be too casual in fielding the ball and the runner will take second. A good base runner is always looking to take that extra base and an outfielder must be quick in his reactions and alert to the possibility of the runner advancing.

No one will take liberties on the bases with the outfielder who charges ground balls well. The best way for an outfielder to field a ground ball is to charge it the same way an infielder would. Don't get down on one knee to field it. Once you are on one knee you are in a locked position and it's extremely difficult to get up quickly and make a throw. The only time you would get down on one knee to field a ball is if it was an extremely hard-hit ball and you had to get down to block it.

The outfielder who doesn't know the condition of the playing field, includ-

38.

ing the position of the sun and the direction of the wind, is asking for trouble. This is especially important since most of the balls fielded are hit into
the air. It is also important to know the condition of the outfield terrain. Is
the grass high and slowing down the ball? Is the ground bumpy and causing
bad hops? Are there any wet spots that might cause him to lose his footing
or slow down the ball?

The best way to test wind direction is to take some grass, throw it into the
air, and see which way it carries. The wind often changes during the course
of a game, however, so it is best to check every inning. Some players like to
check the flag at the park for wind direction, but the flag can be misleading
if you're playing in an enclosed stadium. The flag, which is usually above
the stadium, may be blowing one way, while down on the field the wind may

be going in the opposite direction since the enclosed part of the stadium has created its own air currents. The grass is a safer method.

Every outfielder should get used to wearing sun glasses. Most of the time you can get away without them, but the situation will arise when you will need them, and if you're not used to them, they can be difficult to adjust to.

Modern sun glasses have an adjustable band that fits around the back of the head. When not in use, they are kept in an upright position on the underside of the peak of the cap. When the outfielder wants to bring the glasses down, he just touches the peak of his cap and the glasses drop over his eyes.

If you don't wear sun glasses, the only way to catch a fly ball in the sun is to extend the gloved hand over the head in such a manner that you use the glove as a shield against the sun's rays. The outfielder would then sight the ball either above or below the glove and make the catch at the last possible moment.

Judging fly balls correctly is the hardest thing for a young outfielder to learn. An outfielder must judge fly balls from the sound of the bat against the ball and the speed of the ball in the air. He must anticipate where the ball is going and be there before it arrives. Only through diligent practice can an outfielder become skilled at judging fly balls.

In order to get the fastest start possible in going after a fly ball, the cross-over step is used. If the ball is hit to your right, begin your pursuit by crossing your left foot over your right. The opposite applies on a ball hit to your left.

The toughest ball for an outfielder to judge is the line drive hit over his head. On this play, the outfielder must decide quickly which way to turn. The good outfielder will make this play instinctively, but most outfielders can learn to make the play satisfactorily with practice.

An outfielder should learn to catch the ball with two hands. Nowadays, with the bigger gloves in style many young outfielders, such as Rusty Staub of the Tigers and Amos Otis of the Royals, like to catch the ball one-handed. But this is not a recommended practice since the one-handed catch makes it more difficult to get off a good throw. It takes time to reach up into the glove, take the ball out and throw it. If you catch the ball with two hands, not only is there less chance of your dropping it, but you are in a position to throw it right away.

Always get in the habit of catching the ball the same way every time. The best place to catch a fly ball is off the shoulder of your throwing arm. That way you can catch the ball, get it out of your glove, and throw it all in one motion.

An outfielder should throw the ball overhand and at a low trajectory so that it can be cut off by the infield if necessary. The best type of throw and the easiest to handle is one that bounces once or twice before it reaches the base. The outfielder should grip the ball across the seams in order to get the proper rotation on it. The rotation on the ball should be straight back so that when it hits the ground it will continue in a straight line.

It is very important to keep your throws low so that the cut-off man can handle them. Many young outfielders, especially those with strong arms, often ignore their cut-off men in order to show off their ability. It should be impressed upon them that every time they miss a cut-off man, the runner on first can easily go to second.

There are occasions when you have to overthrow a cut-off man, but that depends on the area in which the ball is hit and the arm of the outfielder. For example, an outfielder with a strong throwing arm might be able to nail a runner quicker at third with a direct, on-the-fly throw to the third baseman than he would if he went through a cut-off man. But he must be sure he can reach the base on the fly a good percentage of the time. If he can only do it 50 per cent of the time, it's not worth the risk.

The center fielder is the one who directs traffic in the outfield. Any time he calls for a ball the other outfielders should give way. The center fielder is the one who has the most area to cover and knows what he can or cannot catch. There are times, such as on a tag play, when one fielder will give way to another who has a stronger arm, even though either outfielder can catch the ball.

The calling of plays is very important in the outfield. Collisions between two outfielders or an outfielder and an infielder occur when there has been a lack of communication between the parties involved.

When a fly ball is hit between two outfielders, the one in the best position to make the play should yell, "I've got it." When an infielder and an outfielder are involved in a play, the outfielder should call the infielder off the play since the outfielder is coming in on the ball and has a better chance of catching it.

If one outfielder is fielding a ball with his back to the infield, the outfielder closest to him is responsible for advising his teammate which base to throw to. At the same time, if one outfielder is chasing a ball near the stands and is unsure of how much room he has, it is up to the outfielder closest to him to advise him on whether to catch it or let it go.

Outfielders should always back up each other, and they are also responsible for backing up the bases on steal attempts, bunt plays, and pick-offs.

SITUATIONS

As we've been trying to stress, anticipation is the key to good defense in baseball. Knowing what to expect in a certain situation and what to do with the ball if you get it are what sets a good infielder apart from a poor one.

To better help acquaint the infielder with the meaning of anticipation, we have outlined some of the more common situations that occur during a

game and have explained the responsibility of each infielder on each particular play.

Sacrifice bunt situation, runner on first—The object here is to try to get that runner at second, if possible. The third baseman, first baseman, and pitcher all charge the bunt. The second baseman covers first and the shortstop covers second. The right fielder backs up first, and the center fielder backs up second (Illustration 40). The catcher would field the ball only if it

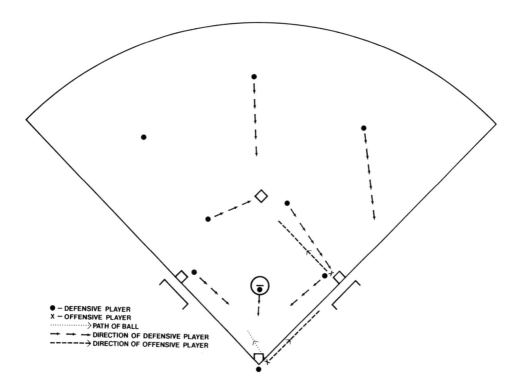

● – DEFENSIVE PLAYER
X – OFFENSIVE PLAYER
·············> PATH OF BALL
→ → → DIRECTION OF DEFENSIVE PLAYER
------→ DIRECTION OF OFFENSIVE PLAYER

40. Playing the sacrifice bunt, runner on first.

is bunted fairly close to home plate. Otherwise, he directs the action by calling out which base to throw to. If the ball is bunted very hard, there is no need for the catcher to call out second base. A play should be made there automatically and without hesitation. Don't look first. Just come up throwing. You must not try for the force at second, however, unless you're fairly certain that you can get the runner.

Sacrifice bunt, runner on second—On this play, the first and second basemen must hold a meeting with the pitcher and decide whether or not they want to try to get the runner at third. If they decide to try for the man at third, the third baseman, instead of charging the bunt, must lay back to cover third base. The responsibility for fielding the ball rests with the pitcher and first baseman. The second baseman must cover first, and the shortstop

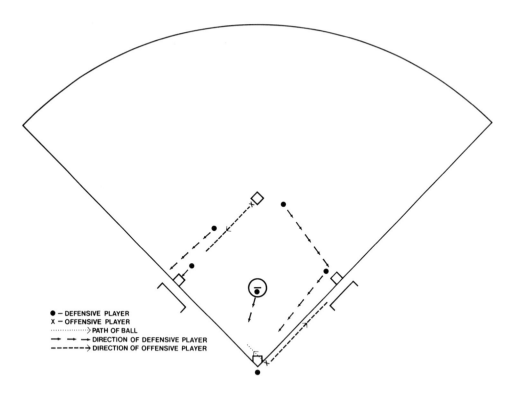

● – DEFENSIVE PLAYER
X – OFFENSIVE PLAYER
··············> PATH OF BALL
→ → →→ DIRECTION OF DEFENSIVE PLAYER
------→ DIRECTION OF OFFENSIVE PLAYER

41. Playing the sacrifice bunt, runner on second.

will back up third base (Illustration 41). Once the second baseman sees the play is being made at third, he must retreat toward second base to guard against the runner advancing past first.

Sacrifice bunt, runners on first and second—This is very similar to the previous situation. Again, a decision must be made among the first baseman, third baseman, and pitcher if they are going to try to get the lead runner. If the batter makes the third baseman field the ball, however, there is no possible way the play can be made at third (Illustration 42). The third baseman then would have to make a quick decision on whether to try for the force at second. If he can get the man at second, that's almost as good as getting the man at third because you would still have a double-play situation for the next batter. A "trick" variation of this play can also be employed with runners on first and second and the batter up obviously intending to sacrifice. The third baseman charges, fields the bunt, turns, and fires to third! The shortstop comes over to take the throw and force the lead runner (Illustration 43). The pitcher and first baseman charge the plate, the second baseman covers first, and the left, center, and right fielders back up third, second, and first base, respectively.

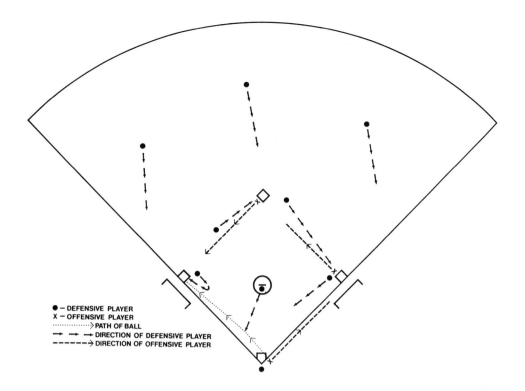

42. Playing the sacrifice bunt, runners on first and second.

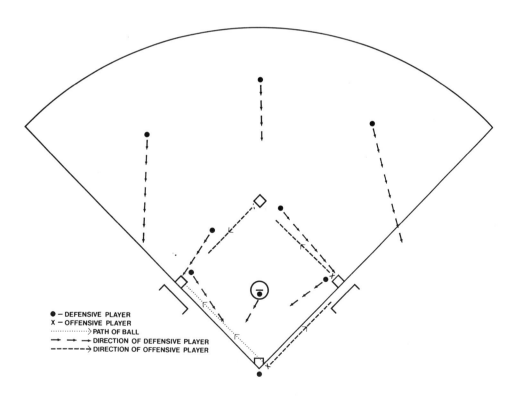

43. Defensive variation for sacrifice bunt situation, runners on first and second.

Bunt, runner on third—This is an impossible play to stop if the runner has a good jump and the ball is bunted on the ground. The third baseman must be especially alert on this play, and if he sees the runner breaking for the plate, he must alert the pitcher and the catcher by yelling it out. The key to defeating the squeeze is to watch the runner. It he breaks for the plate before the pitcher releases the ball, the pitcher should "knock down" the batter and the runner will be caught in a rundown. The defense should be aware of who the batter is before anticipating a squeeze. If it's the third, fourth, or fifth batter, chances of a squeeze are unlikely.

Single to right, runner on first—The second baseman covers second, and the shortstop acts as the cut-off man on the throw from right field to third

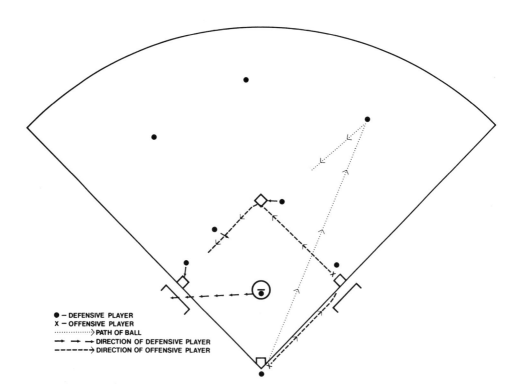

44. Position of second baseman and shortstop on single to right, runner on first.

base (Illustration 44). The shortstop should position himself between short and third on a direct line with the right fielder. The first baseman stays at first and checks to make sure the runner going from first to third has touched second. The pitcher backs up third.

Single to right, runner on second—If the second baseman makes a play for the ball, then the shortstop will cover second. The first baseman serves as the cut-off man on the throw to the plate by positioning himself between first and home about three quarters of the way down the line on a direct line between the right fielder and the catcher (Illustration 45). The third baseman stays at third in case the runner holds, and the second baseman covers first.

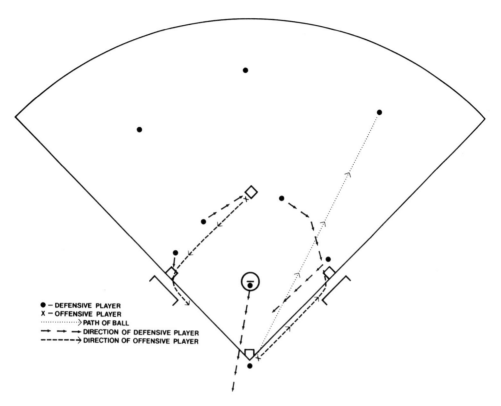

45. Position of fielders on single to right, runner on second.

The pitcher backs up the plate. The first baseman also acts as the cut-off man on a single to center, while the third baseman is the cut-off man on a single to left in the same situation (Illustration 46).

There are certain defensive alignments a team may use in a game to protect a lead or prevent the opposing team from pulling ahead. Here is a look at some of the more common defensive maneuvers:

Drawn-in infield—This is used late in the game when there is a runner on third and the defensive team has a one-run lead it wants to protect, or else trails by one or two runs. In this situation, the infielders move in a few steps closer to home plate from their normal positions so they have a better chance of cutting down the runner at the plate. The use of the drawn-in infield, however, usually depends on who is pitching and who is batting. If there's a pesky hitter at the plate who hits grounders and you have a good low-ball pitcher on the mound, you would probably draw the infield in.

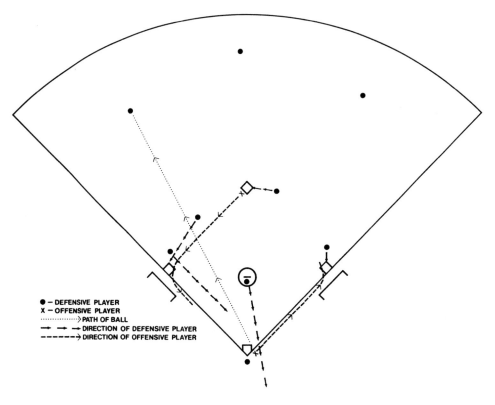

46. Position of fielders on single to left, runner on second.

there's a batter up who hits the ball very hard, it's risky to pull the infield in since it gives him an easier chance of hitting the ball through.

Drawn-in outfield—You would draw the outfield in if the runner on third is the winning run and you know that a deep fly ball would score him anyway. By pulling in the outfield, you attempt to prevent a line drive from falling in safely.

Four-man outfield—Some managers employ this tactic late in a game to guard against an extra-base hit. One of the infielders moves to the outfield and the outfielders spread out to cover as much territory as possible. Moves such as this, however, seldom effect the outcome of a game.

Overshift—This is a tactic employed against strict pull-hitters in which three infielders shift to one side of the diamond, leaving the other infielder to guard the other side of the diamond by himself (Illustrations 47, 48). This often works against pull-hitters who refuse to go to the opposite field with the ball (Ted Williams in his prime was a perfect example), but you can't always rely on the opposing team to be that stubborn. It's the smart player who takes advantage of managerial maneuvers like this.

Six-man infield—Occasionally, a team will use this alignment when they

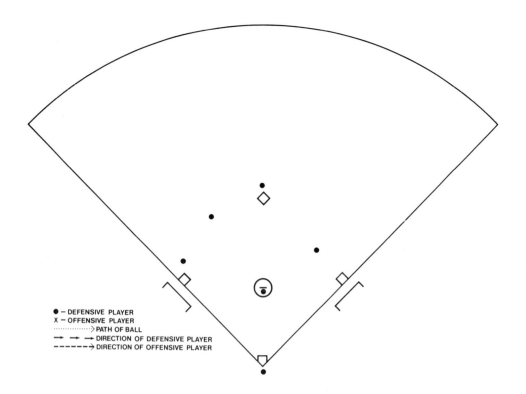

47. *Infield overshift against a righty pull-hitter.*

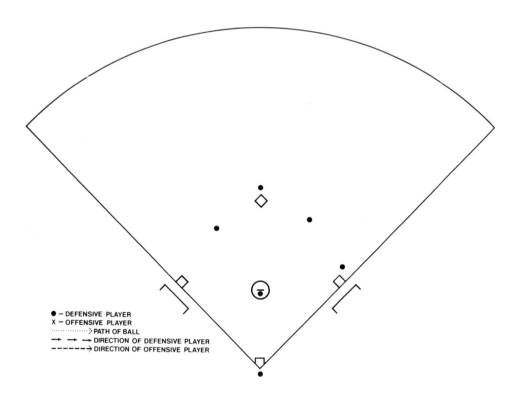

48. *Infield overshift against a lefty pull-hitter.*

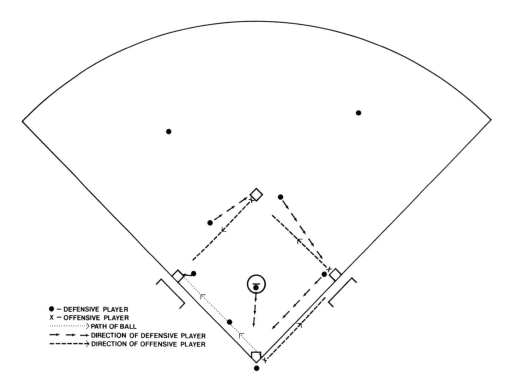

49. Six-man infield alignment in a "sure" sacrifice-bunt situation.

know beyond a doubt that the other team is going to bunt. In this situation, an outfielder is brought in to play one of the infield positions, usually third base, with the third baseman positioning himself about 10 feet away from the plate so he is in a perfect spot to field a bunt (Illustration 49). The idea behind the strategy is to try to get the lead runner. Here again, though, it is wise if the opposing manager goes against the book and has the batter swing away. In this situation, the defense has two men playing unusual and unfa-miliar positions, and the offense would be silly not to try and take advantage of it.

BATTING

Batting is the most difficult task in the game of baseball. It is truly an art form, and not only is it difficult to teach, but it is likewise difficult to learn.

There are two schools of thought on batting. One is that good hitters are born and not made, and that a person cannot be transformed into a good hitter. Another theory, and the more logical one, is that if a batter has good reflexes and co-ordination, he can be taught to be a better hitter by learning to lay off bad pitches, hit the curve ball and hit to the opposite field.

In order to be a good hitter, one should possess good eyesight and the ability to get into a relaxed position at the plate. The latter is most important and should serve as a guide to all coaches. If a player is comfortable at the plate but in a stance that might look awkward, he should be left alone as long as he gets results.

It is not a good idea for a batter or a coach to copy the stance of someone else, even if that person is Hank Aaron or Pete Rose. What is comfortable for Hank Aaron may not be comfortable for you. Batting is an individual thing and everything depends on how comfortable a batter is at the plate. The smart batting coach will make adjustments for each hitter's particular style, and not try to make everyone bat the same way.

Strong arms and wrists are important in becoming a good hitter, and isometric exercises are recommended to build the wrists and forearms so that the batter is able to get the bat around quickly.

Weight lifting, however, is not a recommended form of muscle building. In weight lifting, one has a tendency to build up too much muscle around the shoulders, and instead of adding extra distance to your drives you'll find your ability to get around quickly on the ball has been hampered.

Choosing the proper bat depends largely on a person's size and strength. The size of the bat is determined by the size of your hands and the way the bat feels in them. The weight of the bat depends on your strength and how quickly you can get it around.

Most hitters nowadays are using lighter bats with thin handles. The principle behind this is the same as in golf, whereby the ball goes farther because

50.

the "whip action" creates greater club-head speed. As a result, more home runs are now being hit by smaller players.

A good hitter can be classified as one who makes solid contact with the ball in two out of every five trips to the plate. That doesn't mean he gets a hit two out of every five times, since lots of times a well-hit ball will go right at someone for an out. It means that you have connected on the fat part of the bat twice in every five trips to the plate. The batter who can connect solidly on three of every five trips to the plate falls into the .300-average category.

The key to being a good hitter is being able to "go with" the pitch. That means you have the ability to hit the outside pitch to the opposite field, pull the inside pitch, and hit the pitch across the middle of the plate to center field.

To develop this skill, however, a batter must have: 1) good batting technique; 2) knowledge of the pitcher; 3) knowledge of the strike zone; 4) patience; 5) a good mental attitude.

Batting technique means being comfortable at the plate with a stance that suits you best. No matter what stance you choose, you should keep your head and elbows away from your body so that you can swing easily. You should also be able to see the pitcher clearly.

Where you stand in the batter's box really doesn't matter, but it is important that you be balanced properly with your weight on the balls of your feet and that you be able to reach any ball that is in the strike zone.

The different stances fall into three basic categories—open, normal, and closed. In the open stance, the rear foot is closer to home plate than the front foot and the batter is almost facing the pitcher (Illustration 51). This enables the batter to see the flight of the ball better and helps him handle the inside pitch better.

With the normal, or square, stance, the feet are in a parallel position and the batter is facing directly toward home plate (Illustration 52). This stance gives the batter better plate coverage than the open stance.

In the closed stance, the batter's front foot is closer to home plate than his rear foot, and he is watching the pitcher over his left shoulder (Illustration 53). The closed stance gives the batter much more play with his body, especially with his shoulders. A batter gets a better shoulder turn with this stance and can generate more power.

Once you have selected your stance, the two things you have to concentrate on most to become an effective hitter are stride and hand position.

Striding or stepping into the ball is an important part of hitting. How far a batter strides depends on his stance at the plate, but the thing to avoid is overstriding. Overstriding means taking too long a step toward the pitcher so that you are off balance when you swing. In general, a short stride is preferred because it is easier to maintain good balance, and it keeps your vision steady so that you can better focus on the ball. If a batter has trouble with overstriding, a coach might suggest that the batter widen his stance at the plate, thereby preventing him from taking too big a step.

Hand position is perhaps the most important part of batting. The position of your hands dictates whether or not you can get around properly on the ball. Most young hitters on a high school or college level have very poor hand position. Their hands are held too far back past their shoulders and, consequently, when they stride into the ball they find it difficult to get around on the ball quickly.

51. Open batting stance.

The starting position for the hands should be somewhere within the framework of the body, perpendicular to the chest. When the pitch is delivered and you begin your stride, the hands should move backward in a parallel motion. Now when you swing you are in a position to control the bat, and you are also getting most of your body behind your swing. With your hands too far back at the start, you end up swinging mostly with your arms instead of your body.

Batting requires a perfect co-ordination of shoulders, hips, arms, hands, and wrists. Your shoulders should be level, and the front part of your shoulder should remain pointed at the pitcher until the last possible moment before the swing is made. This delayed action makes it possible to hit curve balls and outside pitches.

52. Normal, or square, batting stance.

Good hip movement is especially important in learning to hit the inside pitch. By pivoting the hips, a batter's shoulders will also turn, enabling him to hit the ball out in front of the plate and pull it.

In swinging, most of the arm power is generated by the back arm, with the forward arm acting as a guide. The arm is extended toward the ball as the bat is snapped, then the wrists and hands are rolled with the top hand crossing over the lower hand.

A good wrist snap is essential in becoming a good hitter. A batter with quick hands and wrists can pull the ball any time he wants, even if he swings late.

As mentioned before, the key to becoming a good hitter is being able to go with the pitch. In learning to go with the pitch, it is important to

53. Closed batting stance.

remember that the front foot is always the guide foot. Whichever way you point that front foot is the way you will hit the ball.

Patience is the key in going with the pitch. A batter must learn to wait on the ball at the plate. Most hitters are too anxious and get around too quickly on the ball. The idea is to wait until the ball is at the plate, then unload.

A person can be a better hitter if he goes up to the plate with the idea that his job is to get the runner on first over to third, and not to knock the ball out of the park. By keeping this in mind, he will learn to go with the pitch instead of trying to pull everything.

Batting practice is a good place to learn the techniques of hitting to the opposite field. The good hitter will work on hitting the ball up the middle or to the opposite field in batting practice instead of trying to hit the ball over the fence. A batter only hurts himself by playing "long ball" in batting practice. Batting practice should be utilized to develop timing, and timing is largely the ability to wait on the ball.

Another thing to remember about batting practice: hitting is constant work and correcting your weaknesses. If you can hit a fast ball, don't always ask for a fast ball in batting practice. Ask for change-ups, curves, sliders, etc. As soon as a pitcher finds out you can hit a particular pitch well, you're not likely to see too many of them in a game. You should be able to hit all types of pitches fairly well, even though you probably will be able to hit some better than others.

A batter should always study the opposing pitcher to learn the types of pitches he throws in certain situations. A good pitcher will always go to his best stuff in a crucial part of the game, and the batter should be aware of what that pitcher's best stuff is.

Some pitchers work by set patterns, and if you see a pitcher often enough you can pick up his patterns. If the pitcher doesn't mix up his pattern and you solve it, then you can usually have success against him.

However, if you're not thinking all the time you're up at the plate, you won't know what the pitcher got you out on. If he's been getting you out on a high fast ball and you continue to swing at the same pitch, then you just aren't concentrating.

Until the pitcher has two strikes on you, you should be anticipating certain pitches. If you're looking for a fast ball and he throws you a curve, you should let the curve go by. Anticipating does not mean you are guessing. A "guess" hitter is one who may be anticipating a certain pitch but will swing anyway no matter what the pitch is.

With two strikes on you, it is important to protect the plate. Choke up on the bat a little or shorten your swing. If you choke up on the bat, you will have better control of it, and with two strikes you should be able to get your bat on the ball no matter where it is.

Knowledge of the strike zone is very important, and it is helpful to know something about the umpire who is calling balls and strikes. All umpires differ in their interpretation of the strike zone, and a batter should know whether the umpire working that particular game is a "low ball" ump or a "high ball" ump. A low-ball umpire tends to call more strikes on low pitches than he does on high ones, and vice-versa for a high-ball umpire. Also, some umps tend to call the inside pitch a little closer than they would an outside one, and vice-versa.

Consequently, you would tend to take fewer low pitches against a low-ball umpire than you would against a high-ball umpire.

The secret to being a good hitter is to hit strikes and not balls, and here again patience is important. Wait for your pitch! Be aggressive, but don't be overanxious. Remember, the ball doesn't have to be right over the heart of the plate to be a good pitch to hit. About 50 per cent of the hits a batter gets in his career are on pitches that are outside the strike zone. You know, of course, what pitches you can handle and what you cannot.

It is always a good idea to take a strike when you face a pitcher for the first time in a game. You have no idea of the pitcher's speed unless you take a pitch. It's even better if you can draw out the count. That way you've probably gotten a chance to see his curve, fast ball, and possibly another pitch, and you know their velocity and effectiveness. The next time up, you'll know more about what to expect, and it should make you a better hitter.

The more pitches you see each time up, the better off you're going to be. There's an old saying that first-ball hitters are your .200 hitters. Your best hitters always hit better with a count on them because they know they'll get good pitches to hit.

No one can be a good hitter unless he has a positive approach to the art. Even if a pitcher has struck you out three times in a row, you must go into that batter's box with the idea that he was lucky and that you're really going to rip the ball.

Batting requires a great deal of concentration, and you should prepare yourself mentally before you get up to the plate. While you're in the dugout before the game, think about who is pitching for the other team and make a mental note of what he throws, what his best pitch is, and what kinds of pitches he's liable to make a mistake on. Does he throw his change-up high? Can you dig in against him? These are some of the things you should be asking yourself before you've reached the plate.

When you move to the on-deck circle as the next batter, familiarize yourself with the game situation. Maybe there's a runner on first and you think you can go to right field on the pitcher. Well, be thinking about it when you get up there and try it.

Remember, a good hitter isn't just a guy who hits for a high average. Batting averages can be deceiving. A good hitter must often sacrifice himself to help the team. That often means hitting behind the runner to move him into scoring position.

Hitting behind the runner differs from the hit-and-run or run-and-hit plays in that all the batter is trying to do is tap the ball toward second base so that the runner can advance to second or third. It is similar to a sacrifice, except that the runner is going on the play and the batter is merely trying to protect him by swinging easily at the ball.

The hit-and-run is a deliberate attempt by the batter to get a base hit while the runner is going by hitting the ball to any field. The hit-and-run sign is given by the batter to the runner, and the batter swings at the pitch, no matter where it is, and tries to hit the ball through the infield.

On the run-and-hit, the manager signals for a steal and it is the batter's responsibility to swing at the pitch. The batter must swing at the ball, no matter where it is, but it is not imperative that he hit it. If he does, fine, but the idea of swinging is merely to make it more difficult for the catcher to throw the runner out.

Most coaches and managers insist that a batter swing at the pitch every time a runner is stealing in order to give the runner the maximum protection possible.

Even when a batter is in the on-deck circle he has an important function. The on-deck batter is responsible for getting the bat of the preceding hitter out of the area near home plate, so that it won't interfere with the runner sliding into home plate or with the catcher trying to make the play.

The on-deck batter also acts as another coach on plays at the plate by signaling the runner to either slide or stand up depending on how close the play is. The raising of both arms over the head is a signal for the runner to stand up, while a downward motion with the arms means the runner should slide. The on-deck batter can also tell the runner which way to slide by moving his arms in a downward motion to either the left or right side.

A little word of encouragement from the on-deck batter to the batter at the plate can also be helpful. At times, the on-deck batter is the only player the hitter can hear when he steps into hit, and a little pep talk can be a real asset—especially against a tough pitcher who has been mowing down the hitters all day.

The on-deck circle is a good spot from which to get a look at the pitcher. Often, from the dugout or the bench, you can't see that well, but from the on-deck circle you can really size-up a pitcher and sometimes spot a flaw that might help you when it's your turn to hit.

BUNTING

An important phase of batting, but unfortunately one that is far too lightly regarded by most players, is bunting. A successful bunt can often mean the difference between winning and losing, yet many players don't work hard enough at developing this skill.

There are three types of bunts—the sacrifice bunt, the bunt for a base hit, and the squeeze bunt.

55. *"Square-around" sacrifice-bunt stance.*

The sacrifice bunt is the one used most often in a game, and its sole purpose is to move the base runner from first to second or second to third so that he is in a better position to score. The sacrifice bunt means exactly what it implies, that the batter is to give himself up so the runner can advance.

There are two schools of thought on the best way to execute a sacrifice bunt. One is the "square-around" theory in which the batter squares his body around so that he is facing the pitcher and slides his top hand up the bat near the label (Illustration 55), then steers the bat from that position. The major criticism of this theory is that the batter is in an unnatural batting position and would be unable to get out of the way should the pitcher throw at him. Many batters have been injured by bunting at the ball in this manner—either by getting hit on the hands by a pitch or by wrenching their backs trying to get out of the way.

The second and more accepted way of bunting is to remain in a normal batting stance and rotate the body by pivoting at the hips. The ball should then be bunted by sliding the top hand up the bat (Illustration 56) or by using a choke-bat grip. Some managers and coaches feel the choke-bat grip, where you keep your hands close together, is preferable because it gives the batter better control of the bat.

The important thing to remember in sacrifice bunting is to lay the bat out in FRONT of the plate. If the bat is in front of the plate, the bunt will be

56. Normal sacrifice-bunt stance.

landing in fair territory. If the batter is too deep in the batter's box, the bat
will not be over the plate and the bunt will go foul.

Where to bunt the ball on a sacrifice depends on who's playing the respective positions. Normally, it's a good policy to try to keep the bunt away from
the pitcher, since he's the closest infielder and could easily turn the bunt into
a force-out. If the third baseman has a "scatter" arm, it might be wise to try
to let him field it in hopes that he will throw the ball away. But, normally,
the best bet is to bunt it at the first baseman, especially if he's right-handed,
since it is very difficult for a right-handed first baseman to make the force
play at second. It is also easier for a right-handed batter to bunt the ball toward first.

With a runner on second, the sacrifice bunt should also be directed at the
first baseman. First basemen are generally the slowest of the infielders and
very few have strong arms. The odds are very high in the batter's favor on
moving the man to third if he bunts toward first, since very few first
baseman have the ability or inclination to try for the out at third.

With runners on first and second, the bunt should be directed at the third
baseman. If he can be made to field the ball, there will be no force play at
third, and he will also be reluctant to throw to second since it means a run if
his throw is wild.

The art of sacrifice bunting should be made a mandatory skill for any pitcher. Pitchers are generally weak hitters because they don't get to take much batting practice, but they can help themselves considerably if they learn to bunt. A pitcher who has learned to execute a sacrifice bunt can often keep himself in a game a lot longer.

The success or failure of bunting for a base hit depends on the element of surprise and the placement of the bunt. Many right-handed batters give themselves away when bunting for a hit by dropping their rear foot before laying down the bunt. Once the third baseman sees the batter make that movement, he will charge quickly and the batter is usually an easy out. It is best to keep the weight balanced as in a normal stance, then shift it to the front foot at the last second before bunting the ball.

In bunting for a base hit, the right-handed batter can either drop the ball down the third-base line or push the ball to the right side in the direction of the second baseman. If the batter chooses to bunt down the third-base line, he should try to keep the ball as close to the line as possible so that the third baseman has a very difficult angle of approach.

Any time the third baseman is playing deep or appears to be back on his heels is a good time to try a bunt. Perhaps he has made the last out of the previous inning and is still thinking about it. Now you've caught him napping and can outsmart him with a bunt.

It's a good idea to try a bunt down the third-base line every now and then just to keep the third baseman honest. Even if the ball goes foul, you've succeeded in making him move in closer to the plate, and that means you won't have to hit the ball as hard to get it through the infield. If you allow the third baseman to play deep all the time he will cut off too many hits.

A "push" bunt is attempted when the batter sees the second baseman playing deep and the first baseman playing close to the line. The idea is to push the ball past the pitcher toward the second baseman, but you must be careful not to get the ball too far to the right where the first baseman can field it. This is a good bunt to use against a left-handed pitcher whose follow-through on his delivery carries him off the mound toward third base.

A left-handed batter has a definite advantage in bunting for a base hit, since he is a step and a half closer to first base at the start. A left-handed batter can either "drag" the ball toward first base or push it toward third base in his attempt to beat out a bunt. The drag bunt is good to try against a pitcher who is not adept at covering first base, or when the first baseman is playing deep. The important thing on a drag bunt is to get the ball past the pitcher's left side.

In executing a drag bunt, the batter uses a crossover step with his rear foot. This means he is transferring his weight from the back foot to the front foot and taking a step toward first base. As his rear foot is about to hit the ground, the batter makes contact with the ball, making sure to roll his top hand so that the ball is pulled toward the right side (Illustration 57).

For some strange reason, most left-handed batters prefer to drag the ball rather than push it toward third, although the push bunt for a left-handed

57. Proper technique for executing the drag bunt.

batter would seem to be a more formidable weapon since he has the extra step and a half and the third baseman must make his throw slightly off balance. On this play the batter uses the crossover step again, but the bat is angled so that the hitting surface faces third (Illustration 58).

The squeeze play can be an effective weapon late in a game where one run can decide the contest, but the success of a squeeze depends greatly on the element of surprise.

There are two types of squeeze plays—suicide and safety—and the choice of either one depends on the game situation. The suicide squeeze is usually reserved for the latter part of the game when there is a runner on third, one out, and the runner is the tying or winning run. The safety squeeze is used to score a runner from third or, where there are runners on first and third, to score the runner from third and advance the runner from first to second.

With the suicide squeeze, the runner on third breaks for the plate when the

58. Proper technique for executing the push bunt.

pitch is thrown and the batter MUST bunt the ball on the ground in fair territory or the runner is a sure out. With the safety squeeze, the runner on third doesn't make his move until the ball has been bunted. On this play, the bunt must be well placed or the runner will not be able to score.

Most coaches prefer the suicide squeeze if they are going to use the maneuver at all. The safety squeeze puts too much emphasis on a well-executed bunt and too much pressure on the runner. With the suicide squeeze, the batter is under pressure to put the ball on the ground, but it does not have to be a perfect bunt.

The suicide squeeze requires perfect teamwork between the runner and the batter. The first thing the batter must do is acknowledge the signal for the squeeze by a prearranged sign such as adjusting his batting helmet with two hands.

Both the batter and the runner must be careful not to give the play away or the runner on third is certain to get picked off. The runner should take a walking lead and not break for the plate until the pitcher's front foot has touched the ground in his delivery toward the plate. Once the pitcher's front foot hits the ground, he cannot change the intended flight of the ball.

However, if the runner moves before the pitcher's foot hits the ground, the pitcher will throw directly at the batter and the runner will be caught. By the same token, the batter must not give any indication that he is going to bunt until the pitcher's front foot hits the ground. The batter must try to bunt the ball regardless of where the pitch is and direct the bunt toward the pitcher to insure its remaining in fair territory.

The suicide squeeze is almost always attempted when the pitcher is behind on the count to the batter to insure a better chance of a strike being bunted at.

BASERUNNING

Speed alone does not make a good base runner. In fact, a player does not have to be especially fast to be a good base runner, but he should be able to make a quick getaway from a starting position and be able to shift into high gear quickly.

Baserunning is dictated by the game situation, and to be a successful base runner a player must always know the number of outs, the position of the outfielders, and the strength and accuracy of their respective throwing arms.

Getting from first to third or from second to home is the aim of every base runner on a base hit, and a runner should know his own capabilities and those of the outfielders.

Before the game starts, every player should take at least one lap around the bases. This serves to loosen up your leg muscles and helps you get the feel of the base paths.

Running to first looks like the easiest part of baseball, but a common fault among many young players is a bad start from home plate. The reason for many bad starts is the batter's insistence on watching where he hits the ball. The player who follows the ball while running to first base decreases his running speed, and many times that is the difference between his being safe or out. All that is needed is a quick glance toward the area the ball was hit while running to first base.

As soon as the batter hits the ball, he should focus his eyes on first base and run as hard as he can. To get out of the batter's box quickly, a right-handed batter should take his first step with his right foot, and a left-handed batter with his left foot.

On a ball fielded by the catcher or pitcher near the first-base line, the runner must run the last 45 feet to first within a designated 3-foot area. If he runs to the outside or inside of that area to block the throw, he will be called out.

Once on first base, a runner has several duties before he takes his lead. First, he should check to see how many outs there are. If there are two out, the runner should be a little more cautious on the bases. On a single, for ex-

59.

ample, he would be foolish to try for third if he thinks it will be a close play since he is in scoring position at second anyway.

Secondly, the runner on first will survey the outfield to see where the outfielders are playing and, thirdly, he will check the third-base coach for any possible signs. All this should be done while he is still standing on the base.

The lead a runner takes off first should be determined by how quickly he can get back to the base should the pitcher throw over there. A runner should be off the base just far enough so that he can get back in time with a head-first dive if he has to.

There are different types of leads a runner can take, but the most common type on an amateur level is the "walking" lead. In this type lead, the runner begins walking slowly off first base as the pitcher comes to a set position. Then, as the pitcher goes into his delivery, the runner, who has not come to a stop, breaks for second.

This often works on an amateur level where pitchers are inexperienced in throwing to first base. On a professional level, however, a pitcher would make the runner come to a stop before delivering his pitch to the plate.

Most runners will take a lead in which they come to a set position with the knees slightly bent, the weight evenly distributed on the balls of the feet, and the eyes focused on the pitcher. In this position they are able to go in either direction equally well.

When a runner is given the sign to steal, he should start his move with the crossover step. In the crossover step, the runner simply pivots on his right foot and crosses his left foot over his right.

Then he pushes off with his right foot, which enables him to get into high gear in an instant. This same principle is used in the stealing of any base.

Base stealing is dependent on a good lead, a quick start, and a good slide. Most base stealing is done on the pitcher, not the catcher, because most pitchers don't bother to keep the runner close to the base and take too much time to release the ball to the plate.

It is easier to steal against a right-handed pitcher than a left-hander because a runner can get a bigger lead against him since a right-hander's back is to first base.

A runner on first base should concern himself with a right-handed pitcher's left knee and left shoulder. On a throw to first base the pitcher bends his left knee slightly in making the pivot, whereas on the throw to the plate his knee is lifted higher. Some pitchers tilt their left shoulders toward first base when working out of the set position, and once that shoulder moves in the direction of home plate it is the signal for the runner to break for second. As soon as the pitcher has moved his shoulder toward home plate, he cannot throw to first without committing a balk.

There are other giveaways a good base stealer will look for. Some pitchers, like former National League star Juan Marichal, have a big leg kick, and their move to first base differs considerably from their move to home plate.

Some pitchers will use a head movement to try to keep the base runner close to the bag, but the good base runner should be concentrating on the pitcher's body movement and not be fooled by his head.

It is harder, of course, to steal against left-handers since they are looking right at you all the time. Some, however, will give themselves away by certain habits, and it is up to the base runner to pick these out.

Sometimes a runner might try a delayed steal of second base, but this is recommended only for the very skilled base runner. A delayed steal should only be tried when the second baseman and the shortstop are playing far away from second base.

In a delayed steal the runner from first doesn't break until the ball reaches the catcher. Since he has not broken on the pitch, the shortshop and second baseman assume there will not be a steal attempt and will not move to cover second base. The slightest tip-off on the part of the runner will, of course, cause the play to fail. But it can be an effective maneuver if timed properly.

A good play—especially in amateur ranks—is the double steal with runners on first and third. In this play the runner on first breaks for second on the pitch, while the runner on third waits to see where the catcher throws the ball. If he throws the ball toward second, the runner from third breaks for the plate if he is sure the throw cannot be cut off by the pitcher. Quite often the shortstop or second baseman will be in front of second base and cut off the throw to make a play at the plate, but if you've timed your move correctly you should be able to beat a return throw to the plate.

The runner on first can help in this situation by stopping midway to second and getting caught in a rundown, thereby allowing the runner on third to score. A delayed double steal is another variation of this play.

Knowing when to steal is as important as knowing how, although very few base runners are given permission to steal on their own. Most of the time the manager will decide when to employ the steal.

During the latter part of a game when a run doesn't mean anything, it is not a good time to steal. Nor is it sound baseball to steal with two out and your big hitter at the plate.

Sliding is one of the most important aspects of stealing and baserunning in general. Yet, unfortunately, there are far too few players today who know how to slide properly.

Proper sliding form includes a complete relaxation of the body as it is falling to the ground. The slide begins about 10 feet from the base, and the body momentum takes the player the rest of the way.

A player's eyes should be focused on the base throughout the entire slide, with the arms and hands extended overhead in most instances.

The fault of many players in sliding is indecision, and this can cause serious injury. Once a player makes up his mind to slide he should go through with it. When a player changes his mind at the last moment, the body cannot adjust and the spikes often jam into the dirt causing muscle pulls—even sprained or broken ankles.

There are three accepted forms of sliding—the hook slide, the feet-first slide, and the bent-leg slide. One other type, the head-first slide, is frowned on by coaches because the injury risk is great. There is no particular advantage to the head-first slide, but there are a lot of disadvantages. There have been instances where players have received serious concussions from being tagged too hard on the head or suffered lacerations of the face from being smacked with the thick lacing of a glove.

The hook slide is perhaps the most graceful-looking of all slides, but even with this slide the injury factor is present. Occasionally, the lead foot gets caught and the momentum of the body causes the leg to give, resulting in a broken leg or ankle.

The principle of the hook slide is to hook the body and legs around the tag so that you catch a corner of the base (Illustration 60). The hook slide can be made to either side of the base, and it's a good idea to vary it. If you slide the same way every time, the infielder will know what to expect and you will find yourself sliding into a tag rather than away from one.

When hook sliding to the right, the take-off is usually off the left foot. The body falls to the right side, both legs are extended straight toward the base with toes pointed out, and the right foot is slightly raised to the right of the base. The left foot and left toes would touch the corner of the base, and the

60. The end of a hook slide.

body would be in a flat position with the hands and arms upraised. Unfortunately, most hook sliders have a tendency to drag their hands, a bad policy which often causes sprained wrists. If your tendency is to drag your hands, it is wise to keep a sponge or some infield dirt in your palms and throw your hands up in the air when you slide.

The feet-first slide is used when the fielder gives no indication of what side he will receive the throw. With this slide, the feet are extended straight out and the slide is made straight toward the center of the base (Illustration 61). It is a fast way of getting to the base and can be made on either the left or right side of the body.

The best slide of all is the bent-leg slide, and many coaches insist that their players adopt this way of sliding. In the bent-leg slide, or sitting-standing slide as it is sometimes called, the runner comes into the base in almost a sitting position and rises to his feet all in one motion. In this slide the body weight is thrown forward with one leg extended straight ahead and the other bent, or tucked, under the extended leg (Illustration 62). The take-off is made off either foot and to either side of the base, and when the extended foot makes contact with the base, the bent leg straightens and the momentum brings the runner to his feet.

One of the major features of this slide is that the injury factor is very small. The slide is made with the toes of the extended foot pulled back so that the heel spikes cannot get caught in the ground. Even if the runner happens to hit the base late, about the worst that could happen to him is a bruised foot.

61. Proper technique for the feet-first slide.

Its best feature, though, is that it enables the runner to get up quickly and advance to another base in case there has been a wild throw. With the hook slide, your body is sprawled on the ground, and by the time you unscramble yourself it's too late to advance another base.

The bent-leg slide is also ideal to use when attempting to prevent the pivot man at second base from completing a double play. This is a function a base runner on first should be conscious of every time he gets on base. However, he must remember that he is allowed to stray only 6 feet to either side of the base when attempting to make contact with the defensive player. The runner can be called out if, in the umpire's judgment, he went beyond the 6-foot limit.

62. Proper technique for the bent-leg slide.

The idea in stopping the pivot man from making the relay to first base is to clip his legs right out from under him just as he is ready to release the ball.

An important facet of baserunning is rounding the bases properly, and the correct way is to hit the inner part of the bag with the left foot. This allows you to make the sharpest turn possible and cuts down the running distance. You should be able to hit the bases very sharply without falling down or losing stride, but it takes practice to get the proper timing down. If you find you cannot touch the base with your left foot without breaking stride, it's all right to touch it with your right foot. But through practice, you'll learn to hit the base with your left foot automatically. It is crucial that you touch each base. Many games have been lost because the runner forgot to touch a base and the oversight was called to the attention of the umpire by an alert infielder.

Many runners, even on a major league level, approach first base at too wide an angle on a base hit. Their angle of approach carries them way over into foul territory, which only serves to increase the distance from home to first.

A runner should take the shortest route possible to first on a base hit, approaching the base just outside the foul line in foul territory. The inner part of the base is touched with the left foot, the body pivots sharply as the runner turns toward second and continues running until the outfielder picks up the ball—usually about 30 feet toward second—or fumbles it—in which case he keeps going for second.

In going from first to third on a single, the runner uses his own judgment if the ball is hit in front of him to left field, and watches the third-base coach if the ball is hit behind him to right field. The only time you would really use the third-base coach is when the ball is hit behind you and you can't see the play develop.

On a ball hit to right field, the runner would pick up the third-base coach after he rounds second base, and the coach's signal would tell him whether or not to hold at second or continue to third. Usually, the waving of the left arm in a circular motion means to continue, while two hands held high over the head means to stop.

A good base runner really doesn't need a coach, however. He knows his own speed better than the coach, and his instincts can tell him whether or not he can beat the throw.

A base runner must be careful at all times not to interfere with an infielder as he is preparing to field a ball. The fielder takes precedence at all times, and a base runner will be called out for interference if he bumps into the fielder on the base line while the fielder is in the act of handling the ball.

When you are running the bases, it is important that you run as fast as you can on every play. Run out all ground balls and flies to the outfield as if you had gotten a hit. Very often, a ball that appears to be a sure out will be misplayed by the defense, and your hustle might pave the way for a big inning. If you loaf on the base paths, it makes you and your team look third rate.

Here's an example of how hustle on the base paths can pay off in a run for your team. Let's say there are runners on first and second and one out and the batter hits what appears to be a sure double-play ball to shortstop. The shortstop throws to second for the force-out, but the relay throw gets by the first baseman. The runner on second rounds third and heads for home while the batter rounds first and heads for second. The first baseman retrieves the ball and throws to second in time to get the runner sliding in for the third out of the inning. However, if the runner on second had crossed the plate before the tag was made at second, the run will count since the double play was not part of a continuation play. If, however, the runner on second has loafed on his way to the plate and does not make it before the tag play at second, then the run will not count.

Getting a good jump when the ball is hit is an essential part of baserunning, and there are various times when you can start moving before the play develops. If there are two out and runners on first and second, or first, second, and third, and there is a 3-2 count on the batter, the runners should be off and running as the pitcher goes into his windup. Also, if there are two out and there is a two-strike count on the batter and he commits himself to swinging at the pitch, the runner should be breaking from the base when he sees the bat come around.

Baserunning is a lot of fun and very challenging. But it takes a long time to develop into a good base runner, and it can be mastered only through hard work.

COACHES

The first- and third-base coaches can play an integral part in the winning or losing of a close game. Their responsibilities differ but their chief duty is to aid the base runner in any way possible.

The first-base coach has less to do than the third-base coach, and his responsibility is mainly that of a "cheerleader." He can aid the batter by instructing him to "make a turn" when a ball falls in safely or is hit high in the

air to the outfield. It is the first-base coach's job to know at all times where the ball is and to instruct the base runner as soon as he reaches first.

Once the runner reaches first, it is the first-base coach's job to alert him to the number of outs and to whatever offensive possibilities may exist. He also instructs him to stay on the base until the pitcher has reached a set position on the mound, and he is responsible for keeping a close eye on the pitcher's move to first base and alerting the runner every time the pitcher throws over to first.

With runners on first and second, or the bases loaded, the first baseman will usually play behind the runner. Then it is the first-base coach's duty to keep an eye on the first baseman so that he doesn't sneak in behind the runner for an attempted pick-off play. The first-base coach's position in this instance would be facing the first baseman, with his back toward home plate.

On fly balls to the outfield, the first-base coach should instruct the runner to go halfway toward second or to tag up, depending on how deep the ball is hit.

As mentioned before, the third-base coach aids the runner going from first to third or from second to home when the runner cannot see the ball. He will also aid the runner on third by reminding him to tag up on a fly ball and not to try to score on a grounder unless it goes through the infield. On a double-steal attempt, the third-base coach will also warn the runner not to go home unless the ball is thrown through to second base.

The third-base coach's most important function is giving signals. He gives all the offensive signals during a game, and it is up to the batter and base runners to look at him repeatedly to get the play that the manager wants used.

INTRODUCTION TO RULES

In order for an athletic event to function properly, there must be a set of rules to determine conduct and govern play on the field.

Since baseball is one of the more complex of games, its rules are strict and diversified.

To better educate the young player in understanding this game, the following section of *Baseball: The Sports Playbook* is devoted to the rules of the game as they appear in the Official Baseball Rules.

We are reprinting those portions of the rules that we feel will be most helpful to the young player. Knowing the rules of the game is as important as knowing the physical actions that are expected of you, the player. A player who understands the rules has a decided advantage over one who does not.

The following excerpts from Official Baseball Rules are reprinted with the permission of the Commissioner of Baseball.

2.00—Definition of Terms.

(All definitions in Rule 2.00 are listed alphabetically; excerpts are shown below.)

An APPEAL is the act of a fielder in claiming violation of the rules by the offensive team.

A BALK is an illegal act by the pitcher with a runner or runners on base, entitling all runners to advance one base.

A BALL is a pitch which does not enter the strike zone in flight and is not struck at by the batter.

A BASE ON BALLS is an award of first base granted to a batter who, during his time at bat, receives four pitches outside the strike zone.

BATTER-RUNNER is a term that identifies the offensive player who has just finished his time at bat until he is put out or until the play on which he became a runner ends.

A BUNT is a batted ball not swung at, but intentionally met with the bat and tapped slowly within the infield.

A CATCH is the act of a fielder in getting secure possession in his hand or glove of a ball in flight and firmly holding it; providing he does not use his cap, protector, pocket or any other part of his uniform in getting possession. It is not a catch, however, if simultaneously or immediately following his contact with the ball, he collides with a player, or with a wall, or if he falls down, and as a result of such collision or falling, drops the ball. It is not a catch if a fielder touches a fly ball which then hits a member of the offensive team or an umpire and then is caught by another defensive player. If the fielder has made the catch and drops the ball while in the act of making a throw following the catch, the ball shall be adjudged to have been caught. In establishing the validity of the catch, the fielder shall hold the ball long enough to prove that he has complete control of the ball and that his release of the ball is voluntary and intentional.

A DEAD BALL is a ball out of play because of a legally created temporary suspension of play.

A DOUBLE PLAY is a play by the defense in which two offensive players are put out as a result of continuous action, providing there is no error between putouts.

(a) A force double play is one in which both putouts are force plays.

(b) A reverse force double play is one in which the first out is a force play and the second out is made on a runner for whom the force is removed by reason of the first out. . . .

A FAIR BALL is a batted ball that settles on fair ground between home and first base, or between home and third base, or that is on or over fair territory when bounding to the outfield past first or third base, or that touches first, second or third base, or that first falls on fair territory on or beyond first base or third base, or that, while on or over fair territory, touches the person of an umpire or player, or that, while over fair territory, passes out of the playing field in flight.

> NOTE: A fair fly shall be judged according to the relative position of the ball and the foul line, including the foul pole, and not as to whether the fielder is on fair or foul territory at the time he touches the ball.

FAIR TERRITORY is that part of the playing field within, and including the first base and third base lines, from home base to the bottom of the playing field fence and perpendicularly upward. All foul lines are in fair territory.

FIELDER'S CHOICE is the act of a fielder who handles a fair grounder and, instead of throwing to first base to put out the batter-runner, throws to another base in an attempt to put out a preceding runner. The term is also used . . . (b) to account for the advance of a runner (other than by stolen base or error) while a fielder is attempting to put out another runner; and (c) to account for the advance of a runner made solely because of the defensive team's indifference. (Undefended steal.)

A FLY BALL is a batted ball that goes high in the air in flight.

A FORCE PLAY is a play in which a runner legally loses his right to occupy a base by reason of the batter becoming a runner.

A FOUL BALL is a batted ball that settles on foul territory between home and first base, or between home and third base, or that bounds past first or third base on or over foul territory, or that first falls on foul territory beyond first or third base, or that, while on or over foul territory, touches the person of an umpire or player, or any object foreign to the natural ground.

> NOTE: A foul fly shall be judged according to the relative position of the ball and the foul line, including the foul pole, and not as to whether the fielder is on foul or fair territory at the time he touches the ball.

FOUL TERRITORY is that part of the playing field outside the first and third base lines extended to the fence and perpendicularly upwards.

A FOUL TIP is a batted ball that goes sharp and direct from the bat to the catcher's hands and is legally caught. It is not a foul tip unless caught and any foul tip that is caught is a strike, and the ball is in play. It is not a catch if it is a rebound, unless the ball has first touched the catcher's glove or hand.

A GROUND BALL is a batted ball that rolls or bounces close to the ground.

The HOME TEAM is the team on whose grounds the game is played, or if the game is played on neutral grounds, the home team shall be designated by mutual agreement.

An ILLEGAL PITCH is (1) a pitch delivered to the batter when the pitcher does not have his pivot foot in contact with the pitcher's plate; (2) a quick return pitch. An illegal pitch when runners are on base is a balk.

An ILLEGALLY BATTED BALL is (1) one hit by the batter with one or both feet on the ground entirely outside the batter's box, or (2) one hit with a bat which does not conform to [the rules].

An INFIELD FLY is a fair fly ball (not including a line drive nor an attempted bunt) which can be caught by an infielder with ordinary effort, when first and second, or first, second, and third bases are occupied, before two are out. The pitcher, catcher, and any outfielder who stations himself in the infield on the play shall be considered infielders for the purpose of this rule.

When it seems apparent that a batted ball will be an Infield Fly, the umpire shall immediately declare "Infield Fly" for the benefit of the runners. If the ball is near the baselines, the umpire shall declare "Infield Fly, if Fair."

The ball is alive and runners may advance at the risk of the ball being caught, or retouch and advance after the ball is touched, the same as on any fly ball. If the hit becomes a foul ball, it is treated the same as any foul.

> NOTE: If a declared Infield Fly is allowed to fall untouched to the ground, and bounces foul before passing first or third base, it is a foul ball. If a declared Infield Fly falls untouched to the ground outside the baseline, and bounces fair before passing first or third base, it is an Infield Fly.

INTERFERENCE

(a) Offensive interference is an act by the team at bat which interferes with, obstructs, impedes, hinders or confuses any fielder attempting to make a play. If the umpire declares the batter, batter-runner, or a runner out for interference, all other runners shall return to the last base that was, in the judgment of the umpire, legally touched at the time of the interference, unless otherwise provided by these rules.

(b) Defensive interference is an act by a fielder which hinders or prevents a batter from hitting a pitch.

(c) Umpire's interference occurs (1) When an umpire hinders, impedes or prevents a catcher's throw attempting to prevent a stolen base, or (2) When a fair ball touches an umpire on fair territory before passing a fielder.

(d) Spectator interference occurs when a spectator reaches out of the stands, or goes on the playing field, and touches a live ball.

On any interference the ball is dead.

THE LEAGUE PRESIDENT shall enforce the official rules, resolve any disputes involving the rules, and determine any protested games. The league president may . . . suspend any player, coach, manager or umpire for violation of these rules, at his discretion.

A LIVE BALL is a ball which is in play.

A LINE DRIVE is a batted ball that goes sharp and direct from the bat to a fielder without touching the ground.

THE MANAGER is a person appointed by the club to be responsible for the team's actions on the field, and to represent the team in communications with the umpire and the opposing team. A player may be appointed manager. . . .

OBSTRUCTION is the act of a fielder who, while not in possession of the ball and not in the act of fielding the ball, impedes the progress of any runner.

OVERSLIDE (or OVERSLIDING) is the act of an offensive player when his slide to a base, other than when advancing from home to first base, is with such momentum that he loses contact with the base.

The PERSON of a player or an umpire is any part of his body, his clothing or his equipment.

A PITCH is a ball delivered to the batter by the pitcher.

The pitcher's PIVOT FOOT is that foot which is in contact with the pitcher's plate as he delivers the pitch.

A QUICK RETURN pitch is one made with obvious intent to catch a batter off balance. It is an illegal pitch.

A RUNNER is an offensive player who is advancing toward, or touching, or returning to any base.

SET POSITION is one of the two legal pitching positions.

SQUEEZE PLAY is a term to designate a play when a team, with a runner on third base, attempts to score that runner by means of a bunt.

A STRIKE is a legal pitch when so called by the umpire, which—

(a) Is struck at by the batter and is missed;

(b) Is not struck at, if any part of the ball passes through any part of the strike zone;

(c) Is fouled by the batter when he has less than two strikes;

(d) Is bunted foul;

(e) Touches the batter as he strikes at it;

(f) Touches the batter in flight in the strike zone; or

(g) Becomes a foul tip.

The STRIKE ZONE is that space over home plate which is between the batter's armpits and the top of his knees when he assumes his natural stance. The umpire shall determine the strike zone according to the batter's usual stance when he swings at a pitch.

TOUCH. To touch a player or umpire is to touch any part of his body, his clothing or his equipment.

A TRIPLE PLAY is a play by the defense in which three offensive players are put out as a result of continuous action, providing there is no error between putouts.

WIND-UP POSITION is one of the two legal pitching positions.

3.00—Game Preliminaries.

3.02 No player shall intentionally discolor or damage the ball by rubbing it with soil, rosin, paraffin, licorice, sand-paper, emery-paper or other foreign substance.

> PENALTY: The umpire shall demand the ball and remove the offender from the game. In case the umpire cannot locate the offender, and if the pitcher delivers such discolored or damaged ball to the batter, the pitcher shall be removed from the game at once and shall be suspended automatically . . .

3.04 A player whose name is on his team's batting order may not become a substitute runner for another member of his team.

3.05 (a) The pitcher named in the batting order handed the umpire-in-chief . . . shall pitch to the first batter or any substitute batter until such batter is put out or reaches first base, unless the pitcher sustains injury or illness which, in the judgment of the umpire-in-chief, incapacitates him from pitching.

(b) If the pitcher is replaced, the substitute pitcher shall pitch to the batter then at bat, or any substitute batter, until such batter is put out or reaches first base, or until the offensive team is put out, unless the substitute pitcher sustains injury or illness which, in the umpire-in-chief's judgment, incapacitates him for further play as a pitcher.

(c) If an improper substitution is made for the pitcher, the umpire shall direct the proper pitcher to return to the game until the provisions of this rule are fulfilled. If the improper pitcher is permitted to pitch, any play that results is legal. The improper pitcher becomes the proper pitcher as soon as he makes his first pitch to the batter, or as soon as any runner is put out.

3.14 Members of the offensive team shall carry all gloves and other equipment off the field and to the dugout while their team is at bat. No equipment shall be left lying on the field, either in fair or foul territory.

3.15 No person shall be allowed on the playing field during a game except players and coaches in uniform, managers, news photographers authorized by the home team, umpires, officers of the law in uniform and watchmen or other employees of the home club. In case of unintentional interference with play by any person herein authorized to be on the playing field, except umpires, the ball is alive and in play. If the interference is intentional, the ball shall be dead at the moment of the interference and the umpire shall impose such penalties as in his opinion will nullify the act of interference.

3.16 When there is spectator interference with any thrown or batted ball, the ball shall be dead at the moment of interference and the umpire shall impose such penalties as in his opinion will nullify the act of interference.

> APPROVED RULING: If spectator interference clearly prevents a fielder from catching a fly ball, the umpire shall declare the batter out.

3.17 Players and substitutes of both teams shall confine themselves to their team's benches unless actually participating in the play or preparing to enter the game, or coaching at first or third base. No one except players, substitutes, managers, coaches, trainers and batboys shall occupy a bench during a game.

> PENALTY: For violation the umpire may, after warning, remove the offender from the field.

4.00—Starting and Ending a Game.

4.03 When the ball is put in play at the start of, or during a game, all fielders other than the catcher shall be on fair territory.
(a) The catcher shall station himself directly back of the plate. He may leave his position at any time to catch a pitch or make a play except that when the batter is being given an intentional base on balls, the catcher must stand with both feet within the lines of the catcher's box until the ball leaves the pitcher's hand.
PENALTY: Balk.
(b) The pitcher, while in the act of delivering the ball to the batter, shall take his legal position;
(c) Except the pitcher and the catcher, any fielder may station himself anywhere in fair territory;
(d) Except the batter, or a runner attempting to score, no offensive player shall cross the catcher's lines when the ball is in play.
4.06 (a) No manager, player, substitute, coach, trainer or batboy shall at any time, whether from the bench, the coach's box or on the playing field, or elsewhere—
(1) Incite, or try to incite, by word or sign a demonstration by spectators;
(2) Use language which will in any manner refer to or reflect upon opposing players, an umpire, or any spectator;

(3) Call "Time," or employ any other word or phrase or commit any act while the ball is alive and in play for the obvious purpose of trying to make the pitcher commit a balk.

(4) Make intentional contact with the umpire in any manner.

(b) No fielder shall take a position in the batter's line of vision, and with deliberate unsportsmanlike intent, act in a manner to distract the batter.

PENALTY: The offender shall be removed from the game and shall leave the playing field, and, if a balk is made, it shall be nullified.

4.07 When a manager, player, coach or trainer is ejected from a game, he shall leave the field immediately and take no further part in that game. He shall . . . either leave the park or take a seat in the grandstand well removed from the vicinity of his team's bench or bullpen.

4.08 When the occupants of a player's bench show violent disapproval of an umpire's decision, the umpire shall first give warning that such disapproval shall cease. If such action continues—

PENALTY: The umpire shall order the offenders from the bench . . . If he is unable to detect the offender, or offenders, he may clear the bench of all substitute players. The manager of the offending team shall have the privilege of recalling to the playing field only those players needed for substitution in the game.

4.09 HOW A TEAM SCORES.

(a) One run shall be scored each time a runner legally advances to and touches first, second, third, and home base before three men are put out to end the inning. EXCEPTION: A run is not scored if the runner advances to home base during a play in which the third out is made (1) by the batter-runner before he touches first base; (2) by any runner being forced out; or (3) by a preceding runner who is declared out because he failed to touch one of the bases.

(b) When the winning run is scored in the last half-inning of a regulation game, or in the last half of an extra inning, as the result of a base on balls, hit batter or any other play with the bases full which forces the runner on third to advance, the umpire shall not declare the game ended until the runner forced to advance from third has touched home base and the batter-runner has touched first base.

PENALTY: If the runner on third refuses to advance and to touch home base in a reasonable time, the umpire shall disallow the run, call out the offending player and order the game resumed. If, with two out, the batter-runner refuses to advance to and touch first base, the umpire shall disallow the run, call out the offending player and order the game resumed. If, before two are out, the batter-runner refuses to advance to and touch first base, the run shall count, but the offending player shall be called out.

5.00—Putting the Ball in Play. Live Ball.

5.06 When a batter becomes a runner and touches all bases legally he shall score one run for his team.

5.08 If a thrown ball accidentally touches a base coach, or a pitched or thrown ball touches an umpire, the ball is alive and in play. However, if the coach interferes with a thrown ball, the runner is out.

5.09 The ball becomes dead and runners advance one base, or return to their bases, without liability to be put out, when—

(a) A pitched ball touches a batter, or his clothing, while in his legal batting position; runners, if forced, advance;

(b) The plate umpire interferes with the catcher's throw; runners may not advance;

> NOTE: The interference shall be disregarded if the catcher's throw retires the runner.

(c) A balk is committed; runners advance (See Penalty 8.05);

(d) A ball is illegally batted; runners return;

(e) A foul ball is not caught; runners return. The umpire shall not put the ball in play until all runners have retouched their bases;

(f) A fair ball touches a runner or an umpire on fair territory before it touches an infielder including the pitcher, or touches an umpire before it has passed an infielder other than the pitcher;

> NOTE: If a fair ball goes through, or by, an infielder, and touches a runner immediately back of him, or touches a runner after being deflected by an infielder, the ball is in play and the umpire shall not declare the runner out. In making such decision the umpire must be convinced that the ball passed through, or by, the infielder and that no other infielder had the chance to make a play on the ball; runners advance, if forced;

(g) A pitched ball passes the catcher and lodges in the umpire's mask or paraphernalia; runners advance;

(h) Any legal pitch touches a runner trying to score; runners advance;

5.10 The ball becomes dead when an umpire calls "Time." The umpire-in-chief shall call "Time"—

(a) When in his judgment weather, darkness or similar conditions make immediate further play impossible;

(b) When light failure makes it difficult or impossible for the umpires to follow the play;

(c) When an accident incapacitates a player or an umpire;

(1) If an accident to a runner is such as to prevent him from proceeding to a base to which he is entitled, as on a home run hit out of the playing field, or an award of one or more bases, a substitute runner shall be permitted to complete the play.

(d) When a manager requests "Time" for substitution, or for a conference with one of his players;

(e) When the umpire wishes to examine the ball, to consult with either manager, or for any similar cause;

(f) When a fielder, after catching a fly ball, falls into a bench or stand, or falls across ropes into a crowd when spectators are on the field. As pertains to runners, the provisions of 7.04 (c) shall prevail.

NOTE: If a fielder after making a catch steps into a bench, but does not fall, the ball is in play and runners may advance at their own peril.

(g) When an umpire orders a player or any other person removed from the playing field. . . .

5.11 After the ball is dead, play shall be resumed when the pitcher takes his place on the pitcher's plate with a new ball or the same ball in his possession and the plate umpire calls "Play." The plate umpire shall call "Play" as soon as the pitcher takes his place on his plate with the ball in his possession.

6.00—The Batter.

6.01 (a) Each player of the offensive team shall bat in the order that his name appears in his team's batting order.

(b) The first batter in each inning after the first inning shall be the player whose name follows that of the last player who legally completed his time at bat in the preceding inning.

6.02 (a) The batter shall take his position in the batter's box promptly when it is his time at bat.

(b) The batter shall not leave his position in the batter's box after the pitcher comes to Set Position, or starts his windup.

PENALTY: If the pitcher pitches, the umpire shall call "Ball" or "Strike," as the case may be.

(c) If the batter refuses to take his position in the batter's box during his time at bat, the umpire shall order the pitcher to pitch, and shall call "Strike" on each such pitch. The batter may take his proper position after any such pitch, and the regular ball and strike count shall continue, but if he does not take his proper position before three strikes are called, he shall be declared out.

6.03 The batter's legal position shall be with both feet within the batter's box.

APPROVED RULING: The lines defining the box are within the batter's box.

6.04 A batter has legally completed his time at bat when he is put out or becomes a runner.

6.05 A batter is out when—

(a) His fair or foul fly ball (other than a foul tip) is legally caught by a fielder;

(b) A third strike is legally caught by the catcher;

(c) A third strike is not caught by the catcher when first base is occupied before two are out;

(d) He bunts foul on third strike;

(e) An Infield Fly is declared;

(f) He attempts to hit a third strike and the ball touches him;

(g) His fair ball touches him before touching a fielder;

(h) After hitting or bunting a fair ball, his bat hits the ball a second time in fair territory. The ball is dead and no runners may advance. If the batter-runner drops his bat and the ball rolls against the bat in fair territory and, in the umpire's judgment, there was no intention to interfere with the course of the ball, the ball is alive and in play;

(i) After hitting or bunting a foul ball, he intentionally deflects the course of the ball in any manner while running to first base. The ball is dead and no runners may advance;

(j) After a third strike or after he hits a fair ball, he or first base is tagged before he touches first base;

(k) In running the last half of the distance from home base to first base, while the ball is being fielded to first base, he runs outside (to the right of) the three-foot line, or inside (to the left of) the foul line, and in the umpire's judgment in so doing interferes with the fielder taking the throw at first base; except that he may run outside (to the right of) the three-foot line or inside (to the left of) the foul line to avoid a fielder attempting to field a batted ball;

(1) An infielder intentionally drops a fair fly ball or line drive, with first, first and second, first and third, or first, second and third base occupied before two are out. The ball is dead and runner or runners shall return to their original base or bases;

> APPROVED RULING: In this situation, the batter is not out if the infielder permits the ball to drop untouched to the ground, except when the Infield Fly rule applies.

(m) A preceding runner shall, in the umpire's judgment, intentionally interfere with a fielder who is attempting to catch a thrown ball or to throw a ball in an attempt to complete any play;

(n) With two out, a runner on third base, and two strikes on the batter, the runner attempts to steal home base on a legal pitch and the ball touches the runner in the batter's strike zone. The umpire shall call "Strike Three," the batter is out and the run shall not count; before two are out, the umpire shall call "Strike Three," the ball is dead, and the run counts.

6.06 A batter is out for illegal action when—

(a) He hits an illegally batted ball;

(b) He steps from one batter's box to the other while the pitcher is in position ready to pitch;

(c) He interferes with the catcher's fielding or throwing by stepping out of the batter's box or making any other movement that hinders the catcher's play at home base. EXCEPTION: Batter is not out if any runner attempting to advance is put out, or if runner trying to score is called out for batter's interference.

(d) He uses or attempts to use a bat that, in the umpire's judgment, has been altered or tampered with in such a way to improve the distance factor or cause an unusual reaction on the baseball. This includes, bats that are filled, flat-surfaced, nailed, hollowed, grooved or covered with a substance such as paraffin, wax, etc.

No advancement on the bases will be allowed and any out or outs made during a play shall stand.

In addition to being called out, the player shall be ejected from the game and may be subject to additional penalties as determined by his League President.

6.07 BATTING OUT OF TURN.

(a) A batter shall be called out, on appeal, when he fails to bat in his proper turn, and another batter completes a time at bat in his place.

    (1) The proper batter may take his place in the batter's box at any time before the improper batter becomes a runner or is put out, and any balls and strikes shall be counted in the proper batter's time at bat.

(b) When an improper batter becomes a runner or is put out, and the defensive team appeals to the umpire before the first pitch to the next batter of either team, or before any play or attempted play, the umpire shall (1) declare the proper batter out; and (2) nullify any advance or score made because of a ball batted by the improper batter or because of the improper batter's advance to first base on a hit, an error, a base on balls, a hit batter or otherwise.

    NOTE: If a runner advances, while the improper batter is at bat, on a stolen base, balk, wild pitch or passed ball, such advance is legal.

(c) When an improper batter becomes a runner or is put out, and a pitch is made to the next batter of either team before an appeal is made, the improper batter thereby becomes the proper batter, and the results of his time at bat become legal.

(d) (1) When the proper batter is called out because he has failed to bat in turn, the next batter shall be the batter whose name follows that of the proper batter thus called out; (2) When an improper batter becomes a proper batter because no appeal is made before the next pitch, the next batter shall be the batter whose name follows that of such legalized improper batter. The instant an improper batter's actions are legalized, the batting order picks up with the name following that of the legalized improper batter.

APPROVED RULINGS. To illustrate various situations arising from batting out of turn, assume a first-inning batting order as follows:

Abel - Baker - Charles - Daniel - Edward - Frank - George - Hooker - Irwin.

PLAY (1). Baker bats. With the count 2 balls and 1 strike, (a) the offensive team discovers the error or (b) the defensive team appeals. RULING: In either case, Abel replaces Baker, with the count on him 2 balls and 1 strike.

PLAY (2). Baker bats and doubles. The defensive team appeals (a) immediately or (b) after a pitch to Charles. RULING: (a) Abel is called out and Baker is the proper batter; (b) Baker stays on second and Charles is the proper batter.

PLAY (3). Abel walks. Baker walks. Charles forces Baker. Edward bats in Daniel's turn. While Edward is at bat, Abel scores and Charles goes to second on a wild pitch. Edward grounds out, sending Charles to third. The defensive team appeals (a) immediately or (b) after a pitch to Daniel. RULING: (a) Abel's run counts and Charles is entitled to second base since these advances were not made because of the improper batter batting a ball or advancing to first base. Charles must return to second base because his advance to third resulted from the improper batter batting a ball. Daniel is called out, and Edward is the proper batter; (b) Abel's run counts and Charles stays on third. The proper batter is Frank.

PLAY (4). With the bases full and two out. Hooker bats in Frank's turn, and triples, scoring three runs. The defensive team appeals (a) immediately, or (b) after a pitch to George. RULING: (a) Frank is called out and no runs score. George is the proper batter to lead off the second inning; (b) Hooker stays on third and three runs score. Irwin is the proper batter.

PLAY (5). After Play (4) (b) above, George continues at bat. (a) Hooker is picked off third base for the third out, or (b) George flies out, and no appeal is made. Who is the proper leadoff batter in the second inning? RULING: (a) Irwin. He became the proper batter as soon as the first pitch to George legalized Hooker's triple; (b) Hooker. When no appeal was made, the first pitch to the leadoff batter of the opposing team legalized George's time at bat.

PLAY (6). Daniel walks and Abel comes to bat. Daniel was an improper batter, and if an appeal is made before the first pitch to Abel, Abel is out, Daniel is removed from base, and Baker is the proper batter. There is no appeal, and a pitch is made to Abel. Daniel's walk is now legalized, and Edward thereby becomes the proper batter. Edward can replace Abel at any time before Abel is put out or becomes a runner. He does not do so, Abel flies out, and Baker comes to bat. Abel was an improper batter, and if an appeal is made before the first pitch to Baker, Edward is out, and the proper batter is Frank. There is no appeal, and a pitch is made to Baker. Abel's out is now legalized, and the proper batter is Baker. Baker walks. Charles is the proper batter. Charles flies out. Now Daniel is the proper batter, but he is on second base. Who is the proper batter? RULING: The proper batter is Edward. When the proper batter is on base, he is passed over, and the following batter becomes the proper batter.

6.08 The batter becomes a runner and is entitled to first base with out liability to be put out (provided he advances to and touches first base) when—

(a) Four "balls" have been called by the umpire;

(b) He is touched by a pitched ball which he is not attempting to hit unless (1) The ball is in the strike zone when it touches the batter, or (2) The batter makes no attempt to avoid being touched by the ball;

> NOTE: If the ball is in the strike zone when it touches the batter, it shall be called a strike, whether or not the batter tries to avoid the ball. If the ball is outside the strike zone when it touches the batter, it shall be called a ball if he makes no attempt to avoid being touched.
>
> APPROVED RULING: When the batter is touched by a pitched ball which does not entitle him to first base, the ball is dead and no runner may advance.

(c) The catcher or any fielder interferes with him. If a play follows the interference, the manager of the offense may advise the plate umpire that he elects to decline the interference penalty and accept the play. Such election shall be made immediately at the end of the play. However, if the batter reaches first base on a hit, an error, a base on balls, a hit batsman, or otherwise, and all other runners advance at least one base, the play proceeds without reference to the interference.

(d) A fair ball touches an umpire or a runner on fair territory before touching a fielder.

> NOTE: If a fair ball touches an umpire after having passed a fielder other

than the pitcher, or having touched a fielder, including the pitcher, the ball is in play.

6.09 The batter becomes a runner when—

(a) He hits a fair ball;

(b) The third strike called by the umpire is not caught, providing (1) first base is unoccupied, or (2) first base is occupied with two out;

(c) A fair ball, after having passed a fielder other than the pitcher, or after having been touched by a fielder, including the pitcher, shall touch an umpire or runner on fair territory;

(d) A fair fly ball passes over a fence or into the stands at a distance from home base of 250 feet or more. Such hit entitles the batter to a home run when he shall have touched all bases legally. A fair fly ball that passes out of the playing field at a point less than 250 feet from home base shall entitle the batter to advance to second base only [Editor's Note: The foregoing is a rule of *major league* baseball. Required distances vary in other leagues.];

(e) A fair ball, after touching the ground, bounds into the stands, or passes through, over or under a fence, or through or under a scoreboard, or through or under shrubbery, or vines on the fence, in which case the batter and the runners shall be entitled to advance two bases;

(f) Any fair ball which, either before or after touching the ground, passes through or under a fence, or through or under a scoreboard, or through any opening in the fence or scoreboard, or through or under shrubbery, or vines on the fence, or which sticks in a fence or scoreboard, in which case the batter and the runners shall be entitled to two bases;

(g) Any bounding fair ball is deflected by the fielder into the stands, or over or under a fence on fair or foul territory, in which case the batter and all runners shall be entitled to advance two bases;

(h) Any fair fly ball is deflected by the fielder into the stands, or over the fence into foul territory, in which case the batter shall be entitled to advance to second base; but if deflected into the stands or over the fence in fair territory, the batter shall be entitled to a home run. However, should such a fair fly be deflected at a point less than 250 feet from home plate, the batter shall be entitled to two bases only. [Editor's Note: The distance referred to above is in force for *major league* baseball. Other leagues' points of reference differ from the above.]

7.00—The Runner.

7.01 A runner acquires the right to an unoccupied base when he touches it before he is out. He is then entitled to it until he is put out, or forced to vacate it for another runner legally entitled to that base.

7.02 In advancing, a runner shall touch first, second, third, and home base in order. If forced to return, he shall retouch all bases in reverse order, unless the ball is dead under any provision of Rule 5.09. In such cases, the runner may go directly to his original base.

7.03 Two runners may not occupy a base, but if, while the ball is alive, two runners are touching a base, the following runner shall be out when tagged. The preceding runner is entitled to the base.

7.04 Each runner, other than the batter, may without liability to be put out, advance one base when—

(a) There is a balk;

(b) The batter's advance without liability to be put out forces the runner to vacate his base, or when the batter hits a fair ball that touches another runner or the umpire before such ball has been touched by, or has passed a fielder, if the runner is forced to advance;

(c) A fielder, after catching a fly ball, falls into a bench or stand, or falls across ropes into a crowd when spectators are on the field;

(d) While he is attempting to steal a base, the batter is interfered with by the catcher or any other fielder.

> NOTE: When a runner is entitled to a base without liability to be put out, while the ball is in play, or under any rule in which the ball is in play after the runner reaches the base to which he is entitled, and the runner fails to touch the base to which he is entitled before attempting to advance to the next base, the runner shall forfeit his exemption from liability to be put out, and he may be put out by tagging the base or by tagging the runner before he returns to the missed base.

7.05 Each runner including the batter-runner may, without liability to be put out, advance—

(a) To home base, scoring a run, if a fair ball goes out of the playing field in flight and touches all bases legally; or if a fair ball which, in the umpire's judgment, would have gone out of the playing field in flight, is deflected by the act of a fielder in throwing his glove, cap, or any article of his apparel;

(b) Three bases, if a fielder deliberately touches a fair ball with his cap, mask or any part of his uniform detached from its proper place on his person. The ball is in play and the batter may advance to home base at his peril;

(c) Three bases, if a fielder deliberately throws his glove at and touches a fair ball. The ball is in play and the batter may advance to home base at his peril.

(d) Two bases, if a fielder deliberately touches a thrown ball with his cap, mask or any part of his uniform detached from its proper place on his person. The ball is in play;

(e) Two bases, if a fielder deliberately throws his glove at and touches a thrown ball. The ball is in play;

(f) Two bases, if a fair ball bounces or is deflected into the stands outside the first or third base foul lines; or if it goes through or under a field fence, or through or under a scoreboard, or through or under shrubbery or vines on the fence; or if it sticks in such fence, scoreboard, shrubbery or vines;

(g) Two bases when, with no spectators on the playing field, a thrown ball goes into the stands, or into a bench (whether or not the ball rebounds into the field), or over or under or through a field fence, or on a slanting part of the screen above the backstop, or remains in the meshes of a wire screen protecting spectators. The ball is dead. When such wild throw is the first play by an infielder, the umpire, in awarding such bases, shall be governed by the position of the runners at the time the ball was pitched; in all other cases the umpire shall be governed by the position of the runners at the time the wild throw was made;

APPROVED RULING: If all runners, including the batter-runner, have advanced at least one base when an infielder makes a wild throw on the first play after the pitch, the award shall be governed by the position of the runners when the wild throw was made.

(h) One base, if a ball, pitched to the batter, or thrown by the pitcher from his position on the pitcher's plate to a base to catch a runner, goes into a stand or a bench, or over or through a field fence or backstop. The ball is dead;

APPROVED RULING: When a wild pitch or passed ball goes through or by the catcher, or deflects off the catcher, and goes directly into the dugout, stands, above the break, or any area where the ball is dead, the awarding of bases shall be one base. One base shall also be awarded if the pitcher while in contact with the rubber, throws to a base, and the throw goes directly into the stands or into any area where the ball is dead.

If, however, the pitched or thrown ball goes through or by the catcher or through the fielder, and remains on the playing field, and is subsequently kicked or deflected into the dugout, stands or other area where the ball is dead, the awarding of bases shall be two bases from position of runners at the time of the pitch or throw.

(i) One base, if the batter becomes a runner on Ball Four or Strike Three, when the pitch passes the catcher and lodges in the umpire's mask or paraphernalia.

NOTE: If the batter becomes a runner on a wild pitch which entitles the runners to advance one base, the batter-runner shall be entitled to first base only.

7.06 When obstruction occurs, the umpire shall call or signal "Obstruction."

(a) If a play is being made on the obstructed runner, or if the batter-runner is obstructed before he touches first base, the ball is dead and all runners shall advance, without liability to be put out, to the bases they would have reached, in the umpire's judgment, if there had been no obstruction. The obstructed runner shall be awarded at least one base beyond the base he had last legally touched before the obstruction. Any preceding runners, forced to advance by the award of bases as the penalty for obstruction, shall advance without liability to be put out.

(b) If no play is being made on the obstructed runner, the play shall proceed until no further action is possible. The umpire shall then call "Time" and impose such penalties, if any, as in his judgment will nullify the act of obstruction.

7.07 If, with a runner on third base and trying to score by means of a squeeze play or a steal, the catcher or any other fielder steps on, or in front of home base without possession of the ball, or touches the batter or his bat, the pitcher shall be charged with a balk, the batter shall be awarded first base on the interference and the ball is dead.

7.08 Any runner is out when—

(a) (1) He runs more than three feet away from a direct line between bases to avoid being tagged, unless his action is to avoid interference with a fielder fielding a batted ball; or (2) after touching first base, he leaves the baseline, obviously abandoning his effort to touch the next base;

> APPROVED RULING: When a batter becomes a runner on third strike not caught, and starts for his bench or position, he may advance to first base at any time before he enters the bench. To put him out, the defense must tag him or first base before he touches first base.

(b) He intentionally interferes with a thrown ball; or hinders a fielder attempting to make a play on a batted ball;

(c) He is tagged, when the ball is alive, while off his base. EXCEPTION: A batter-runner cannot be tagged out after overrunning or oversliding first base if he returns immediately to the base;

> APPROVED RULING: (1) If the impact of a runner breaks a base loose from its position, no play can be made on that runner at that base if he had reached the base safely.
>
> APPROVED RULING: (2) If a base is dislodged from its position during a play, any following runner on the same play shall be considered as touching or occupying the base if, in the umpire's judgment, he touches or occupies the point marked by the dislodged bag.

(d) He fails to retouch his base after fair or foul ball is legally caught before he, or his base, is tagged by a fielder. He shall not be called out for failure to retouch his base after the first following pitch, or any play or attempted play. This is an appeal play;

(e) He fails to reach the next base before a fielder tags him or the base, after he has been forced to advance by reason of the batter becoming a runner. However, if a following runner is put out on a force play, the force is removed and the runner must be tagged to be put out. The force is removed as soon as the runner touches the base to which he is forced to advance, and if he overslides or overruns the base, the runner must be tagged to be put out. However, if the forced runner, after touching the next base, retreats for any reason toward the base he had last occupied, the force play is reinstated, and he can again be put out if the defense tags the base to which he is forced;

(f) He is touched by a fair ball in fair territory before the ball has touched or passed an infielder. The ball is dead and no runner may score, nor runners advance, except runners forced to advance. EXCEPTION: If a runner is touching his base when touched by an Infield Fly, he is not out, although the batter is out;

NOTE: If runner is touched by an Infield Fly when he is not touching his base, both runner and batter are out.

(g) He attempts to score on a play in which the batter interferes with the play at home base before two are out. With two out, the interference puts the batter out and no score counts;

(h) He passes a preceding runner before such runner is out;

(i) After he has acquired legal possession of a base, he runs the bases in reverse order for the purpose of confusing the defense or making a travesty of the game. The umpire shall immediately call "Time" and declare the runner out;

(j) He fails to return at once to first base after overrunning or oversliding that base. If he attempts to run to second he is out when tagged. If, after overrunning or oversliding first base he starts toward the dugout, or toward his position, and fails to return to first base at once, he is out, on appeal, when he or the base is tagged;

(k) In running or sliding for home base, he fails to touch home base and makes no attempt to return to the base, when a fielder holds the ball in his hand, while touching home base, and appeals to the umpire for the decision.

7.09 It is interference by a batter or a runner when—

(a) After a third strike he hinders the catcher in his attempt to field the ball;

(b) After hitting or bunting a fair ball, his bat hits the ball a second time in fair territory. The ball is dead and no runners may advance. If the batter-runner drops his bat and the ball rolls against the bat in fair territory and, in the umpire's judgment, there was no intention to interfere with the course of the ball, the ball is alive and in play;

(c) He intentionally deflects the course of a foul ball in any manner;

(d) Before two are out and a runner on third base, the batter hinders a fielder in making a play at home base; the runner is out;

(e) Any member or members of the offensive team stand or gather around any base to which a runner is advancing, to confuse, hinder or add to the difficulty of the fielders. Such runner shall be declared out for the interference of his teammate or teammates;

(f) Any batter or runner who has just been put out hinders or impedes any following play being made on a runner. Such runner shall be declared out for the interference of his teammate;

(g) If, in the judgment of the umpire, a base runner wilfully and deliberately interferes with a batted ball or a fielder in the act of fielding a batted ball with the obvious intent to break up a double play, the ball is dead. The umpire shall call the runner out for interference and also call out the batter-runner because of the action of his teammate. In no event may bases be run or runs scored because of such action by a runner.

(h) If, in the judgment of the umpire, a batter-runner wilfully and deliberately interferes with a batted ball or a fielder in the act of fielding a batted ball, with the obvious intent to break up a double play, the ball is dead; the umpire shall call the batter-runner out for interference and shall also call out the runner who had advanced closest to the home plate regardless where the double play might have been possible. In no event shall bases be run because of such interference.

(i) In the judgment of the umpire, the base coach at third base, or first base, by touching or holding the runner, physically assists him in returning to or leaving third base or first base.

(j) With a runner on third base, the base coach leaves his box and acts in any manner to draw a throw by a fielder;

(k) In running the last half of the distance from home base to first base while the ball is being fielded to first base, he runs outside (to the right of) the three-foot line, or inside (to the left of) the foul line and, in the umpire's judgment, interferes with the fielder taking the throw at first base, or attempting to field a batted ball;

(l) He fails to avoid a fielder who is attempting to field a batted ball, or intentionally interferes with a thrown ball, provided that if two or more fielders attempt to field a batted ball, and the runner comes in contact with one or more of them, the umpire shall determine which fielder is entitled to the benefit of this rule, and shall not declare the runner out for coming in contact with a fielder other than the one the umpire determines to be entitled to field such a ball;

(m) A fair ball touches him on fair territory before touching a fielder. If a fair ball goes through, or by, an infielder, and touches a runner immediately back of him, or touches the runner after having been deflected by a fielder, the umpire shall not declare the runner out for being touched by a batted ball. In making such decision the umpire must be convinced that the ball passed through, or by, the infielder, and that no other infielder had the chance to make a play on the ball. If, in the judgment of the umpire, the runner deliberately and intentionally kicks such a batted ball on which the infielder has missed a play, then the runner shall be called out for interference.

PENALTY FOR INTERFERENCE: The runner is out and the ball is dead.

7.10 Any runner shall be called out, on appeal when—

(a) After a fly ball is caught, he fails to retouch his original base before he or his original base is tagged;

(b) With the ball in play, while advancing or returning to a base, he fails to touch each base in order before he, or a missed base, is tagged.

APPROVED RULING: (1) No runner may return to touch a missed base after a following runner has scored. (2) When the ball is dead, no runner may return to touch a missed base or one he has left after he has advanced to and touched a base beyond the missed base.

(c) He overruns or overslides first base and fails to return to the base immediately, and he or the base is tagged;

(d) He fails to touch home base and makes no attempt to return to that base, and home base is tagged.

Any appeal under this rule must be made before the next pitch, or any play or attempted play. If the violation occurs during a play which ends a half-inning, the appeal must be made before the defensive team leaves the field.

An appeal is not to be interpreted as a play or an attempted play.

Successive appeals may not be made on a runner at the same base. If the defensive team on its first appeal errs, a request for a second appeal on the same runner at the same base shall not be allowed by the umpire. (*Intended meaning of the word "err" is that the defensive team in making an appeal threw the ball out of play. For example, if the pitcher threw to first base to appeal and threw the ball into the stands, no second appeal would be allowed.*)

> NOTE: Appeal plays may require an umpire to recognize an apparent "fourth out." If the third out is made during a play in which an appeal play is sustained on another runner, the appeal play decision takes precedence in determining the out. If there is more than one appeal during a play that ends a half-inning, the defense may elect to take the out that gives it the advantage. For the purposes of this rule, the defensive team has "left the field" when the pitcher and all infielders have left fair territory on their way to the bench . . .

7.11 The players, coaches or any member of an offensive team shall vacate any space (including both dugouts) needed by a fielder who is attempting to field a batted or thrown ball.

> PENALTY: Interference shall be called and the batter or runner on whom the play is being made shall be declared out.

7.12 Unless two are out, the status of a following runner is not affected by a preceding runner's failure to touch or retouch a base. If, upon appeal, the preceding runner is the third out, no runners following him shall score. If such third out is the result of a force play, neither preceding nor following runners shall score.

8.00—The Pitcher.

8.01 Legal pitching delivery. There are two legal pitching positions, the Windup Position and the Set Position, and either position may be used at any time.

Pitchers shall take signs from the catcher while standing on the rubber.

(a) The Windup Position. The pitcher shall stand facing the batter, his entire pivot foot on, or in front of and touching and not off the end of the pitcher's plate, and the other foot free. From this position any natural movement associated with his delivery of the ball to the batter commits him to the pitch without interruption or alteration. He shall not raise either foot from the ground, except that in his actual delivery of the ball to the batter, he may take one step backward, and one step forward with his free foot.

NOTE: When a pitcher holds the ball with both hands in front of his body, with his entire pivot foot on, or in front of and touching but not off the end of the pitcher's plate, and his other foot tree, he will be considered in a Windup Position.

(b) The Set Position. Set Position shall be indicated by the pitcher when he stands facing the batter with his entire pivot foot on, or in front of, and in contact with, and not off the end of the pitcher's plate, and his other foot in front of the pitcher's plate, holding the ball in both hands in front of his body and coming to a complete stop. From such Set Position he may deliver the ball to the batter, throw to a base or step backward off the pitcher's plate with his pivot foot. Before assuming Set Position, the pitcher may elect to make any natural preliminary motion such as that known as "the stretch." But if he so elects, he shall come to Set Position before delivering the ball to the batter. After assuming Set Position, any natural motion associated with his delivery of the ball to the batter commits him to the pitch without alteration or interruption.

(c) At any time during the pitcher's preliminary movements and until his natural pitching motion commits him to the pitch, he may throw to any base provided he steps directly toward such base before making the throw.

(d) If the pitcher makes an illegal pitch with the bases unoccupied, it shall be called a ball unless the batter reaches first base on a hit, an error, a base on balls, a hit batter or otherwise.

(e) If the pitcher removes his pivot foot from contact with the pitcher's plate by stepping backward with that foot, he thereby becomes an infielder and if he makes a wild throw from that position, it shall be considered the same as a wild throw by any other infielder.

8.02 The pitcher shall not—

(a) (1) Bring his pitching hand in contact with his mouth or lips while in the . . . circle surrounding the pitching rubber.

> PENALTY: For violation of this part of the rule the umpires shall immediately call a ball. However, if the pitch is made and a batter reaches first base on a hit, an error, a hit batsman or otherwise, and no other runner is put out before advancing at least one base, the play shall proceed without reference to the violation. Repeated offenders shall be subject to [disciplinary action] by the league president.

(2) Apply a foreign substance of any kind to the ball;

(3) expectorate on the ball, either hand or his glove;

(4) rub the ball on his glove, person or clothing;

(5) deface the ball in any manner;

(6) deliver what is called the "shine" ball, "spit" ball, "mud" ball or "emery" ball. The pitcher, of course, is allowed to rub the ball between his bare hands.

> PENALTY: For violation of any part of this rule (8.02 (a) (2 to 6)) the umpire shall:
> (a) Call the pitch a ball, warn the pitcher and have announced . . . the reason for the action.

(b) In the case of a second offense by the same pitcher in the same game, the pitcher shall be disqualified from the game.

(c) If a play follows the violation called by the umpire, the manager of the offense may advise the plate umpire that he elects to accept the play. Such election shall be made immediately at the end of the play. However, if the batter reaches first base on a hit, an error, a base on balls, a hit batsman, or otherwise, and no other runner is put out before advancing at least one base, the play shall proceed without reference to the violation.

(d) Even though the offense elects to take the play, the violation shall be recognized and the penalties in (a) and (b) will still be in effect.

(e) The umpire shall be sole judge on whether any portion of this rule has been violated.

(b) Have on his person, or in his possession, any foreign substance. For such infraction of this section (b) the penalty shall be immediate ejection from the game.

(c) Intentionally delay the game by throwing the ball to players other than the catcher, when the batter is in position, except in an attempt to retire a runner.

> PENALTY: If, after warning by the umpire, such delaying action is repeated, the pitcher shall be removed from the game.

(d) Intentionally pitch at the batter. If, in the umpire's judgment, such violation occurs, the umpire shall warn the pitcher and the manager of the defense that another such pitch will mean immediate expulsion of the pitcher. If such pitch is repeated during the game, the umpire shall eject the pitcher from the game.

8.03 When a pitcher takes his position at the beginning of each inning, or when he relieves another pitcher, he shall be permitted to pitch not to exceed eight preparatory pitches to his catcher during which play shall be suspended. A league by its own action may limit the number of preparatory pitches to less than eight preparatory pitches. Such preparatory pitches shall not consume more than one minute of time. If a sudden emergency causes a pitcher to be summoned into the game without any opportunity to warm up, the umpire-in-chief shall allow him as many pitches as the umpire deems necessary.

8.04 When the bases are unoccupied, the pitcher shall deliver the ball to the batter within 20 seconds after he receives the ball. Each time the pitcher delays the game by violating this rule, the umpire shall call "Ball."

> NOTE: The intent of this rule is to avoid unnecessary delays. The umpire shall insist that the catcher return the ball promptly to the pitcher, and that the pitcher take his position on the rubber promptly. Obvious delay by the pitcher should instantly be penalized by the umpire.

8.05 If there is a runner, or runners, it is a balk when—

(a) The pitcher, while touching his plate, makes any motion naturally associated with his pitch and fails to make such delivery;

(b) The pitcher, while touching his plate, feints a throw to first base and fails to complete the throw;

(c) The pitcher, while touching his plate, fails to step directly toward a base before throwing to that base;

(d) The pitcher while touching his plate, throws, or feints a throw to an unoccupied base, except for the purpose of making a play;

(e) The pitcher makes an illegal pitch;

(f) The pitcher delivers the ball to the batter while he is not facing the batter;

(g) The pitcher makes any motion naturally associated with his pitch while he is not touching the pitcher's plate;

(h) The pitcher unnecessarily delays the game;

(i) The pitcher, without having the ball, stands on or astride the pitcher's plate or while off the plate, he feints a pitch;

(j) The pitcher, after coming to a legal pitching position, removes one hand from the ball other than in an actual pitch, or in throwing to a base;

(k) The pitcher, while touching his plate, accidentally or intentionally drops the ball;

(l) The pitcher, while giving an intentional base on balls, pitches when the catcher is not in the catcher's box;

(m) The pitcher delivers the pitch from Set Position without coming to a stop;

> PENALTY: The ball is dead, and each runner shall advance one base without liability to be put out, unless the batter reaches first on a hit, an error, a base on balls, a hit batter, or otherwise, and all other runners advance at least one base, in which case the play proceeds without reference to the balk.
>
> APPROVED RULING: In cases where a pitcher balks and throws wild, either to a base or to home plate, a runner or runners may advance beyond the base to which he is entitled at his own risk.
>
> APPROVED RULING: A runner who misses the first base to which he is advancing and who is called out on appeal shall be considered as having advanced one base for the purpose of this rule.

8.06 A professional league shall adopt the following rule pertaining to the visit of the manager or coach to the pitcher:

(a) This rule limits the number of trips a manager or coach may make to any one pitcher in any one inning; (b) A second trip to the same pitcher in the same inning will cause this pitcher's automatic removal; (c) The manager or coach is prohibited from making a second visit to the mound while the same batter is at bat, but (d) if a pinch-hitter is substituted for this batter, the manager or coach may make a second visit to the mound, but must remove the pitcher.

A manager or coach is considered to have concluded his visit to the mound when he leaves the . . . circle surrounding the pitcher's rubber.

Notes—Case Book—Comment

The following notes, interpretations and approved rulings are a part of the Official Rules.

(The Following unnumbered official notes apply to paragraphs identified by definitions in Rule 2.00.)

BALL. If the pitch touches the ground and bounces through the strike zone it is a "ball." If such a pitch touches the batter, he shall be awarded first base. If the batter swings at such a pitch after two strikes, the ball cannot be caught, for the purposes of Rule 6.05 (c) and 6.09 (b). If the batter hits such a pitch, the ensuing action shall be the same as if he hit the ball in flight.

FAIR BALL. If a fly ball lands in the infield between home and first base, or home and third base, and then bounces to foul territory without touching a player or umpire and before passing first or third base, it is a foul ball; or if the ball settles on foul territory or is touched by a player on foul territory, it is a foul ball. If any fielder fields such a foul ball in foul territory and throws the ball to first base, the batter is not out. If a fly ball lands on or beyond first or third base and then bounces to foul territory, it is a fair hit.

Clubs, increasingly, are erecting tall foul poles at the fence line with a wire netting extending along the side of the pole on fair territory above the fence to enable the umpires more accurately to judge fair and foul balls. The custom should become universal.

FORCE PLAY. Confusion regarding this play is removed by remembering that frequently the "force" situation is removed during the play. Example: Man on first, one out, ball hit sharply to first baseman who touches the bag and batter-runner is out. The force is removed at that moment and runner advancing to second must be tagged. If there had been a runner on third or second, and either of these runners scored before the tag-out at second, the run counts. Had the first baseman thrown to second and the ball then had been returned to first, the play at second was a force out, making two outs, and the return throw to first ahead of the runner would have made three outs. In that case, no run would score.

Example: NOT A FORCE OUT. One out. Runner on first and third. Batter flies out. Two out. Runner on third tags up and scores. Runner on first tries to retouch before throw from fielder reaches first baseman, but does not get back in time and is out. Three outs. If, in umpire's judgment, the runner from third touched home base before the ball was held at first base, the run counts.

FOUL BALL. Approved Ruling: The exact position of the ball determines whether it is foul or fair, not the position of the fielder's body when he touches the ball.

Approved Ruling: Without touching a fielder, a batted ball hits pitcher's rubber and rebounds over catcher's head, or to foul territory between home and first, or between home and third base. This is a foul.

OFFENSIVE INTERFERENCE. (a) In the event the batter-runner has not reached first base, all runners shall return to the base last occupied at the time of the pitch.

PITCH. Distinguished clearly the difference between a pitch and a thrown ball. A pitch is exclusively the delivery of the ball to the batter. All other deliveries of the ball by one player to another are thrown balls.

3.04 This rule is intended to eliminate the practice of using so-called courtesy runners. No player in the game shall be permitted to act as a courtesy runner for a teammate. No player who has been in the game and has been taken out for a substitute shall return as a courtesy runner. Any player not in the lineup, if used as a runner, shall be considered as a substitute player.

4.09 Baseball is so genuinely a team game that an error of omission, as well as an error of commission, can, and frequently does, nullify the brilliant play of a team-mate.

APPROVED RULING: No run shall score during a play in which the third out is made by the batter-runner before he touches first base. EXAMPLE: One out, Jones on second, Smith on first. The batter, Brown, hits safely. Jones scores. Smith is out on the throw to the plate. Two outs. But Brown missed first base. The ball is thrown to first, an appeal is made, and Brown is out. Three outs. Since Jones crossed the plate during a play in which the third out was made by the batter-runner before he touched first base, Jones' run does not count.

Approved Ruling: Following runners are not affected by an act of a preceding runner unless two are out.

Example: One out, Jones on second, Smith on first, and batter, Brown, hits home run inside the park. Jones fails to touch third on his way to the plate. Smith and Brown score. The defense holds the ball on third, appeals to umpire, and Jones is out. Smith's and Brown's runs count.

Approved Ruling: Two out, Jones on second, Smith on first and batter, Brown, hits home run inside the park. All three runs cross the plate. But Jones missed third base, and on appeal is declared out. Three outs. Smith's and Brown's runs are voided. No score on the play.

Approved Ruling: One out, Jones on third, Smith on second. Batter Brown flies out to center field. Two out. Jones scores after catch and Smith scores on bad throw to plate. But Jones, on appeal, is adjudged to have left third before the catch and is out. Three outs. No runs.

Approved Ruling: Two out, bases full, batter hits home run over fence. Batter, on appeal, is declared out for missing first base. Three outs. No run counts.

Here is a general statement that covers:

When a runner misses a base and a fielder holds the ball on a missed base, or on the base originally occupied by the runner if a fly ball is caught, and appeals for the umpire's decision, the runner is out when the umpire sustains the appeal; all runners may score if possible, except that with two out the runner is out at the moment he misses the bag, if an appeal is made, as applied to the following runners.

Approved Ruling: One out, Jones on third, Smith on first, and Brown flies out to right field. Two outs. Jones tags up and scores after the catch. Smith attempted to return to first but the right fielder's throw beat him to the base. Three outs. But Jones had scored before the throw to catch Smith reached first base, hence Jones' run counts. It was not a force play.

5.06 A run legally scored cannot be nullified by subsequent action of the runner, such as but not limited to an effort to return to third base in the belief that he had left the base before a caught fly ball.

5.09 (f) If a fair ball touches an umpire working in the infield after it has bounded past, or over, the pitcher, it is a dead ball. If a batted ball is deflected by a fielder in fair territory and hits a runner or an umpire while still in flight and then caught by an infielder it shall not be a catch, but the ball shall remain in play.

6.02 (b) The batter leaves the batter's box at the risk of having a strike delivered and called, unless he requests the umpire to call "Time." The batter is not at liberty to step in and out of the batter's box at will.

Once a batter has taken his position in the batter's box, he shall not be permitted to step out of the batter's box in order to use the resin or the pine tar rag, unless there is a delay in the game action or, in the judgment of the umpires, weather conditions warrant an exception.

Umpires will not call "Time" at the request of the batter or any member of his team once the pitcher has started his windup or has come to a set position even though the batter claims "dust in his eyes," "steamed glasses," "didn't get the sign" or for any other cause.

Umpires may grant a hitter's request for "Time" once he is in the batter's box, but the umpire should eliminate hitters walking out of the batter's box without reason. If umpires are not lenient, batters will understand that they are in the batter's box and they must remain there until the ball is pitched.

If pitchers delay once the batter is in his box and the umpire feels that the delay is not justified he may allow the batter to step out of the box momentarily.

If after the pitcher starts his wind-up or comes to a "set position" with a runner on, he does not go through with his pitch because the batter has stepped out of the box, it shall not be called a balk. Both the pitcher and the batter have violated a rule and the umpire shall call time and both the batter and pitcher start over from "scratch."

6.05 (a) See Rule 2.00—CATCH. Catch is legal if ball is finally held by any fielder, even though juggled, or held by another fielder before it touches the ground. Runners may leave their bases the instant the first fielder touches the ball. A fielder may reach over a fence, railing, rope or other line of demarcation to make a catch. He may jump on top of a railing, or canvas that may be in foul ground. No interference should be allowed when a fielder reaches over a fence, railing, rope or into a stand to catch a ball. He does so at his own risk.

6.05 (b) "Legally caught" means in the catcher's glove before the ball touches the ground. It is not legal if the ball lodges in his clothing or paraphernalia; or if it touches the umpire and is caught by the catcher on the rebound.

6.05 (m) The objective of this rule is to penalize the offensive team for deliberate, unwarranted, unsportsmanlike action by the runner in leaving the baseline for the obvious purpose of crashing the pivot man on a double play, rather than trying to reach the base. Obviously this is an umpire's judgment play.

6.07 The umpire shall not direct the attention of any person to the presence in the batter's box of an improper batter. This rule is designed to require constant vigilance by the players and managers of both teams.

7.01 If a runner legally acquires title to a base, and the pitcher assumes his pitching position, the runner may not return to a previously occupied base.

7.04 (b) A runner forced to advance without liability to be put out may advance past the base to which he is entitled only at his peril. If such a runner, forced to advance, is put out for the third out before a preceding runner, also forced to advance, touches home plate, the run shall score.

7.05 (b-c-d-e) The thrown glove or detached cap or mask, etc., must touch the ball. There is no penalty if the ball is not touched.

7.05 (c-e) This penalty shall not be invoked against a fielder whose glove is carried off his hand by the force of a batted or thrown ball, or when his glove flies off his hand as he makes an obvious effort to make a legitimate catch.

7.05 (g) In certain circumstances it is impossible to award a runner two bases. Example: Runner on first. Batter hits fly to short right. Runner holds up between first and second and batter comes around first and pulls up behind him. Ball falls safely. Outfielder, in throwing to first, throws ball into stand.

APPROVED RULING: Since no runner, when the ball is dead, may advance beyond the base to which he is entitled, the runner originally on first base goes to third base and the batter is held at second base.

7.06 The catcher, without the ball in his possession, has no right to block the pathway of the runner attempting to score. The baseline belongs to the runner and the catcher should be there only when he is fielding a ball or when he already has the ball in his hand.

7.08 (b) A runner who is adjudged to have hindered a fielder who is attempting to make a play on a batted ball is out whether it was intentional or not. If, however, the runner has contact with a legally occupied base when he hinders the fielder, he shall not be called out unless, in the umpire's judgment, such hindrance, whether it occurs on fair or foul territory, is intentional. If the umpire declares the hindrance intentional, the following penalty shall apply: With less than two out, the umpire shall declare both the runner and batter out. With two out, the umpire shall declare the batter out.

7.08 (d) Runners need not "tag up" on a foul tip. They may steal on a foul tip. If a so-called foul tip is not caught, it becomes an ordinary foul. Runners then return to their bases.

7.08 (e) and (j) Oversliding and overrunning situations arise at bases other than first base. For instance, before two are out, and runners on first and second, or first, second and third, the ball is hit to an infielder who tries for the double play. The runner on first beats the throw to second base but overslides the base. The relay is made to first base and the batter-runner is out. The first baseman, seeing the runner at second base off the bag, makes the return throw to second and the runner is tagged off the base. Meanwhile runners have crossed the plate. The question is: Is this a force play? Was the force removed when the batter-runner was out at first base? Do the runs that crossed the plate during this play and before the third out was made when the runner was tagged at second, count? Answer: The runs score. It is not a force play. It is a tag play.

7.08 (f) If two runners are touched by the same fair ball, only the first one is out because the ball is instantly dead.

7.09 (e) and (f) If the batter or a runner continues to advance after he has been put out, he shall not by that act alone be considered as confusing, hindering or impeding the fielders.

7.10 (a) "Retouch," in this rule, means to tag up and start from a contact with the base after the ball is caught. A runner is not permitted to take a flying start from a position in back of his base.

8.01 Pitchers must take signs from the catcher while standing on the rubber. Signs shall not be taken while the pitcher is straddling or standing behind the rubber.

Pitchers may disengage the rubber after taking their signs but may not step quickly onto the rubber and pitch. This may be judged a quick pitch by the umpire. When the pitcher disengages the rubber, he must drop his hands to his sides.

Pitchers will not be allowed to disengage the rubber after taking each sign. This will defeat the purpose of Official Baseball Rule 8.01 which was put into the rules to establish uniformity in taking signs while on the rubber in all professional leagues.

8.01 (a) WINDUP POSITION. The pitcher must have both feet squarely on the ground and his entire pivot foot must be on, or in front of and in contact with, the front edge of the pitcher's rubber preliminary to pitching. The rules permit the pitcher to have one foot, not the pivot foot, off the rubber and any distance he may desire back of a line which is an extension of the back edge of the pitcher's plate, but not at either side of the pitcher's plate.

With his "free" foot the pitcher may take one step backward and one step forward, but under no circumstances, to either side, that is to either the first base or third base side of the pitcher's rubber.

NOTE. If a pitcher holds the ball with both hands in front of his body, with his entire pivot foot on or in front of and touching but not off the end of the pitcher's plate, and his other foot free, he will be considered in a windup position.

From this position he may:

(1) deliver the ball to the batter, or

(2) step and throw to a base in an attempt to pick-off a runner or

(3) disengage the rubber (if he does he must drop his hands to his sides).

In disengaging the rubber the pitcher first must step off with his pivot foot and not his free foot first.

He may not go into a set or stretch position—if he does it is a balk.

8.01   (b)   SET POSITION. Preparatory to coming to a set position, the pitcher shall have one hand on his side; from this position he shall go to his set position as defined in Rule 8.01 (b) without interruption and in one continuous motion.

The whole width of the foot in contact with the rubber must be on the rubber. A pitcher cannot pitch from off the end of the rubber with just the side of his foot touching the rubber.

The pitcher, following his stretch, must (a) hold the ball in both hands in front of his body and (b) come to a complete stop. This must be enforced. Umpires should watch this closely. Pitchers are constantly attempting to "beat the rule" in their efforts to hold runners on bases and in cases where the pitcher fails to make a complete "stop" called for in the rules, the umpire should immediately call a "Balk."

8.01   (c)   The pitcher shall step "ahead of the throw." A snap throw followed by the step directly toward the base is a balk.

8.01   (d)   A ball which slips out of a pitcher's hand and crosses the foul line shall be called a ball; otherwise it will be called no pitch. This would be a balk with men on base.

8.01   (e)   The pitcher, while off the rubber, may throw to any base. If he makes a wild throw, such throw is the throw of an infielder and what follows is governed by the rules covering a ball thrown by a fielder.

8.02   (a)   . . . If at any time the ball hits the rosin bag it is in play. In the case of rain or wet field, the umpire may instruct the pitcher to carry the rosin bag in his hip pocket. A pitcher may use the rosin bag for the purpose of applying rosin to his bare hand or hands. Neither the pitcher nor any other player shall dust the ball with the rosin bag; neither shall the pitcher nor any other player be permitted to apply rosin from the bag to his glove, or dust any part of his uniform with the rosin bag.

8.02   (d)   To pitch at a batter's head is unsportsmanlike and highly dangerous. It should be—and is—condemned by everybody. Umpires should act without hesitation in enforcement of this rule.

Gil McDougald

Following his ten-year career as an infielder with the New York Yankees, Gil McDougald was the head baseball coach at Fordham University in New York. During his career in the major leagues, he played on eight Yankee World Series teams and was chosen to the American League All-Star team on five occasions.

McDougald has the distinction of being the only player ever named to an All-Star team at three different positions—second base, shortstop, and third base. His single in the 1957 All-Star Game at Baltimore drove in the winning run, giving the American League a 4–3 triumph.

A native of San Francisco, McDougald attended the University of San Francisco for one year before signing with the Yankees in 1948. He reached the major leagues in 1951 and batted .306 to win Rookie of the Year honors in the American League. In the World Series that year he hit a grand-slam homer and helped the Yankees beat the New York Giants in six games.

McDougald finished his major league career with a .276 lifetime batting average. He retired after the 1960 season, and aside from his tenure in the early '70s at Fordham, he has devoted his full time to his interest in a maintenance company in New Jersey. McDougald resides in Tenafly, N.J.

Fred McMane

Fred McMane is a sportswriter for United Press International. He has been employed by UPI since 1964, and has reported on baseball since '66. He is a former high school letter winner in baseball and is a member of the Baseball Writers Association of America.

A graduate of Rutgers University in New Brunswick, New Jersey, McMane served two years in the Navy as the sports editor of a weekly newspaper before joining UPI.

During his years at the wire service, he has written frequently for sports magazines.